SAMMO HUNG
The Portly Kicker
Introduction by Rick Baker

Sammo Hung (born 7 January 1952), also known as Hung Kam-bo (洪金寶). Sammo is one of the pivotal figures who spearheaded the Hong Kong New Wave movement of the 1980s, helped reinvent the martial arts genre and started the vampire-like genre. He is widely credited with assisting many of his compatriots, giving them their starts in the Hong Kong film industry, by casting them in the films he produced, or giving them roles in the production crew.

Both Sammo Hung and Jackie Chan were often addressed as "Dai Goh", meaning Big Brother, until the filming of Project A, which featured both actors. As Hung was the eldest of the kung fu "brothers", and the first to make a mark on the industry, he was given the nickname "Dai Goh Dai", meaning, Big, Big Brother, or Biggest Big Brother. Sammo Hung recently celebrated his 70th birthday, celebrating a career that has spanned over the past 7 decades.

He was enrolled into a Peking Opera School

as a small boy, run by the disciplined Master Yu Jim Yuen, this was where he would hone all the skills he would need to make him a global star in the world of Kung Fu cinema. In them days, students would normally enrol for the lengthy period of 10 years. Students would perform gruelling tasks, for up to 18 hours a day, including training in the Martial Arts, weapons training, acrobatics, acting and singing. This would of course unite the famous seven to be called "The Seven Little Fortunes" Sammo Hung, Jackie Chan, Yuen Biao, Yuen Wah, Corey Yuen, Yuen Tak and Yuen Mo. They took the first name "Yuen" in a sign of respect for their teacher whilst attending Peking Opera, many kept that first name but others like

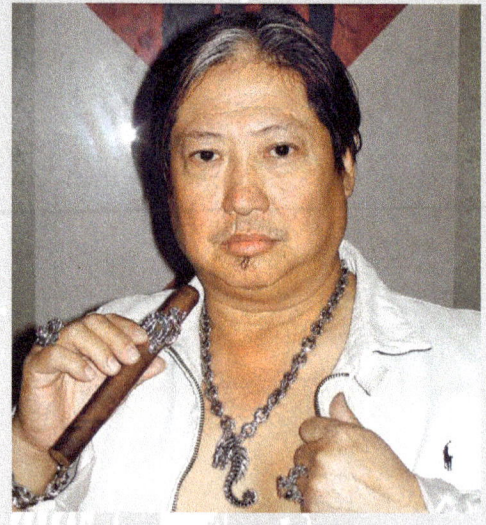

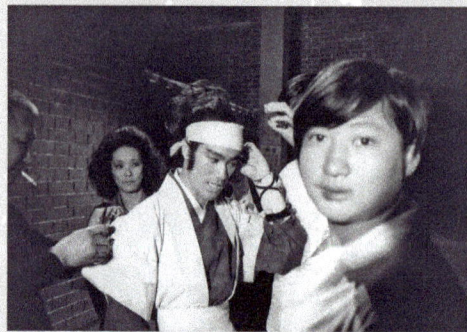

Sammo Hung and Jackie broke away from tradition which was probably frowned upon by Master Yuen.
They would travel and perform to the public, one of the venues being Lai Chi Kok Amusement Park, you can also see a few seconds of the 7 little fortunes performing in a movie called "I Spy", which shows Sammo and the others performing at a festival. They would also be sent out to studios as child actors including Shaw Brothers to perform as extras.
All of the Fortunes have enjoyed success within the movie industry, but Both Jackie and Sammo have excelled becoming A-List stars in their given profession.
No matter who I talk to, about any martial arts movie star, everyone loves Sammo Hung and will have at least half a dozen of his movies in there collection. Eastern Condors one of my all-time top 5 movies, and was very influential in creating my company Eastern Heroes back in 1988. And I was lucky enough to interview

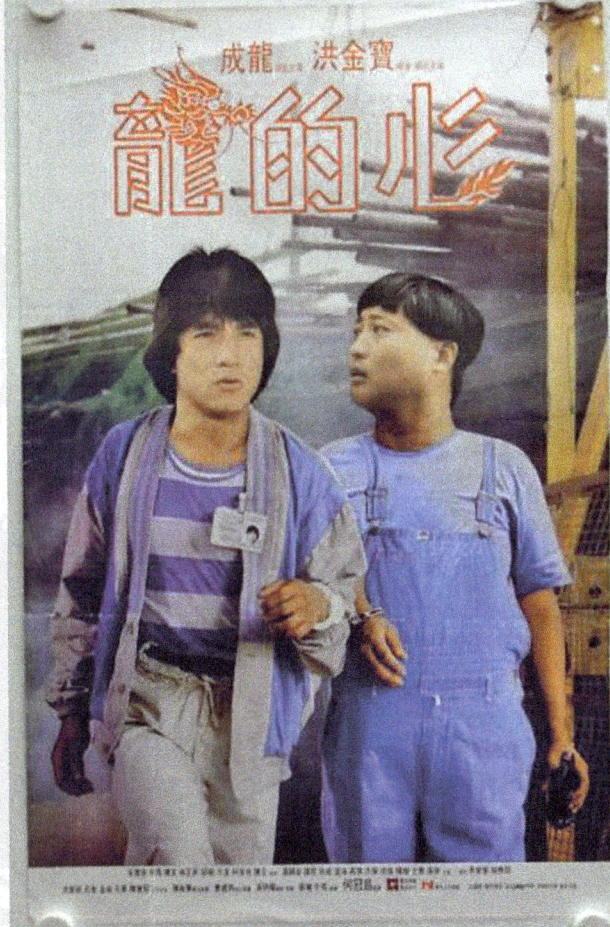

him many years ago at his then Bojon Films Company that he had set in 1989. Prior to this Sammo had set up several other companies. 1980 he saw Raymond Chow pull one of His films from local cinemas after just two weeks. Sammo responded by starting his own production company, Bo Ho Film Company Ltd, allowing him to have greater control to produce Hong Kong films. While Bo Ho produced the movies, Golden Harvest still operated as distributors. His production created a great catalogue of 40 films, several of which Sammo starred in including Encounters of the Spooky Kind (1980), Heart of Dragon (1985), Where's Officer Tuba? (1986) and, Millionaires Express (1986).
In 1983, Hung co-founded another production company, D&B Films Company Ltd ("D&B" being short for "Duk-Bo"), with Dickson Poon and John Shum The company operated until 1992 and produced a total of 77 Hong Kong films including Brandon Lee's Legacy of Rage (1986) Michelle Yeoh's Magnificent Warriors (1987) Cynthia Rothrock in Yes, Madam (1985) and Donnie Yen in Tiger Cage (1988)

One of the memorable moments when entering his office to interview him, firstly! I spotted Yuen Biao who I am a genuine massive fan of. Then as we sat down at a table I glanced to the right of me, and in another room Sammo Hung was holding court with some of the cast for the Movie "Don't Give a Dam". As I stared at the many faces Wang Lung-wei looked directly back at me staring and rather than acknowledge me by giving me a nod of his head, he took two paces and pushed the door that slowly closed denying me to witness what was going on. It so Reminded of the final scene between Michael and Kay, in the "Godfather" when she sees Al Pacino now the new Don holding court with his men, and has Kay looks on one of his soldiers steps forward to restrict her from seeing what is taking place. That day is still one of the most memorable days for me meeting your hero who were informed spoke little English but in fact gave the whole interview in English, Yuen Biao how ever gave his interview in Cantonese, luckily Toby who was with me translated. On that note 28 years on from that meeting, here I am still a huge fan, still following his career and now doing a Sammo Special! Interviewing, those that have worked alongside him, showing their respect for this larger than life action star. Sammo I am happy to say is still active today, even though his health has left him a little

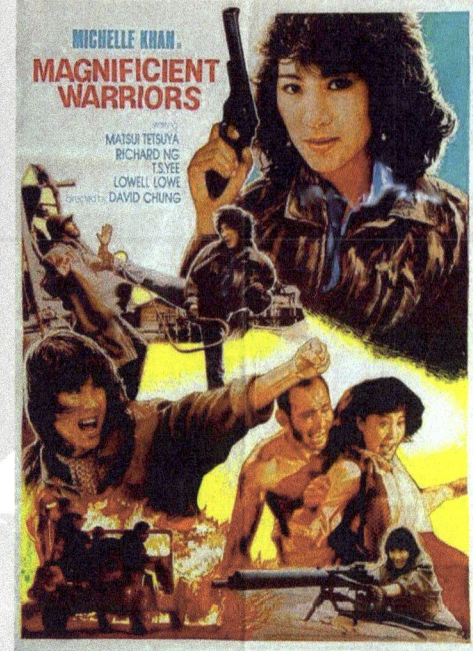

more fragile to be on screen delivering the stunts and the fight action that made him a household name.

He is still a tour de force in the film industry and his popularity is stronger today than it ever was with the re-mastering of his many great classics and next year Warner brother will be celebrating the 50th anniversary of Enter the Dragon.

So even as Sammo Hung enters his twilight years his incredible back catalogue of films will continually keep him in the public eye for many years to come.

So enjoy the issue and Sammo Hung we Salute you.

Poster created & designed by
Tim Hollingsworth

MR NICE GUY
Richard NORTON
李察羅頓

**Interview with Richard Norton
By Rick Baker**

Richard Norton is a world renown Australian martial artist who has attained a 10th Degree in Zen Do Kai Martial Arts, a style he co-founded in Australia, an 8th Degree in the Chuck Norris System, a level 6 in Benny 'The Jet' Urquidez' Ukidokan Kick Boxing and a 5th Degree Black belt in Brazilian Jiu Jitsu under the legendary Machado Bros. He is also an inductee in the Australasian Martial Arts Hall of fame. On top of that he is action film star, stunt/fight coordinator with 45 years in the entertainment industry and has shared the big screen with some of the world's best known martial art stars, including Jackie Chan, Chuck Norris, Cynthia Rothrock, Yasuaki Kurata, Benny the Jet and the legendary Sammo Hung.

To cap off that impressive CV, Richard also worked for 25 years as a personal bodyguard to some of Rock'n'roll's elites, protecting high profile stars like The Rolling Stones, Linda Ronstadt, James Taylor, David Bowie, ABBA, John Belushi, Fleetwood Mac and Stevie Nicks.

Richard recently kindly took time out of filming on the latest Mad Max, 'Furiosa' shoot, to talk about his career and his experience working alongside Sammo Hung.

RB: I was born in 1960, so only got into martial arts through the Bruce Lee craze in the mid 70's. Was that the same for you?

RN: No, I was already well into my Martial Arts journey by then, as I started doing judo in 1961. It all started where I lived in Croydon, a suburb outside of Melbourne and there was a new kid who moved into the house opposite. We soon became friends and I noticed he was disappearing a couple of nights a week when we should have been playing pool, so I asked him where he was going and he told me he was taking Judo classes', which immediately caused my ears to prick up. I immediately asked if I could join him, so his dad would drive us to a nearby suburb, Nunawading, where a local policeman was teaching the classes in a rented hall. A few years later, another friend of ours from High School, who also trained Judo with us, told us about a Karate demonstration that was to take place, near to where we lived. At the time, I'd not really heard much about karate, except from one of Mas Oyama's early books that a friend of mine had. I also remember reading ads for Judo on the back of comic books and that was pretty much the only martial art I really knew of in Australia at the time. Anyway, I eagerly said that we should all go and take a look. The demonstration was of Goju-Kai karate and headed by Tino Ceberano, a Hawaiian Filipina who'd only been in Australia for about six months and who would later be referred to as the 'Father of Australian Karate'. I remember watching him and some white belt students and being mesmerised and thinking, "OMG, this is what I want to do with my life". As an 11-year-old, I was such a skinny kid and basically cannon fodder for the bigger lads in the judo class, so I saw Karate as more about agility and speed and a stand-off art that didn't rely so much on

strength. I immediately joined and started training under Tino Hanshi in 1965/66. This is where my real martial arts journey began and where I met my future partner in the arts, Bob Jones. In 1970, Bob wanted to start his own eclectic MA style and wanted me to go with him. Bob already had an incredible reputation in the Security Business and wanted a style based in tradition, but also catering for the reality of the streets, that we would encounter working the doors of various rough clubs in Melbourne at the time. We basically took the 'blinkers' off and included Boxing, Wresting and Muay Thai into the students training and called our system, 'Zen-Do-Kai'.

RB: That's a bit like Bruce's Jeet Kune Do, in a way.

RN: Yes, we were the Australian pioneers to what we now call MMA, as we embraced whatever fighting arts would work in the real world.

RB: Did you get influenced by the Bruce Lee craze?

RN: Yes, of course. I can't imagine a martial artist at that time that wasn't influenced in some way by Bruce Lee. At one point, Bob Jones and I, had over 500 schools throughout Australia. They were the days when the idea of karate was very new and ad mystical connotations about it. Bruce was an incredible catalyst for students joining us. We were all influenced by his speed and athleticism, and how he mixed styles. Just recently, Guro Dan Inosanto told me that even in 1969; Bruce was working on single and double leg takedowns, which was a good indication of how innovative he was. I mean no traditional stand-up martial artist was considering wrestling in their training.

RB: I remember going to my first kung fu class. There was a queue! All we wanted to do was the theatrical stuff we saw on Enter the Dragon.

RN: We were well established by then and used to do demonstrations at local movie theatre screenings of 'Enter the Dragon'.

RB: Fantastic! Did that lead you onto doing bodyguard work?

RN: That was all through my partner, Bob Jones, and our extensive network of MA schools. In 1972, we had done security for the Sunbury Pop Festival, Australia's version of 'Woodstock'. The promoter was a well-known entrepreneur, Paul Dainty. After the festival, Paul had called us, and asked Bob and I if we would work as personal bodyguards for The Rolling Stones during their tour of Australia. That's how it started. I ended up in that line of work for a long time, over 25 years. After a tour in the late 1970's, Linda Ronstadt asked me to come and work for her full time in California. I remember being quite hesitant at the time, as I was very settled with my MA schools and a local girlfriend, etc. The 'kicker' was when Linda said to me, 'Why don't you try it. You can always go back home?' So that was it. I decided to step out of my comfort zone and off I went. That's what got me over to the US and started my movie career. Another factor was that around the same time, Bob had persuaded Chuck Norris to visit Australia and demonstrate his karate at some kickboxing matches that Bob had started in Australia. I was also demonstrating weapons skills on the same card as Chuck. Anyway, we immediately hit it off and established an immediate friendship. He told me to please get in touch if I ever went to California and we could do some training. What an invitation for a skinny little kid from Croydon. Of course, he was the first person I called when I got there and we ended up training every morning at his house, six days a week for many years. That's how my movie career started, when Chuck asked me if I'd be interested in playing his nemesis, 'Kyo', in a movie he was prepping at the time, 'The Octagon'. That kickstarted everything.

RB: Had you wanted to star in films prior to that?

RN: No. I hadn't aspired to be in movies all. I had once doubled for an actor in a fight scene in a 1976 Australian movie about outback opal miners called, 'The Last of the Knucklemen'. I remember loving the experience but didn't think it was the start of a new career. I know my passion for movies started with working out with Chuck in his backyard, figuring out the fights, weapons training and then then being on set with amazing martial artists like Tadashi Yamashita, Simon and Phillip Rhee and Gerald Okamura, whose careers were then in their infancy. Yes, that's what made the difference. I mean I was actually

being paid to involve my passion and to do something I loved, as well as meeting all these phenomenal people. So, then a friend and former student of Chuck's, Pat Johnson, told me about a movie that was in development called, 'Force: Five', and that I should audition for one of the leads. I remember I walked in and there were about one hundred amazing martial artists demonstrating their skills and vying for a part.

RB: Is that when you first met Benny the Jet?

RN: No, I'd already met him through Chuck and was regularly training with him at his brother, Arnold's house, in the SF Valley. This was way before the world famous 'Jet Center' was established.

RB: I really rate him as a fighter.

RN: He's still one of the few real role models for me. Whenever I get the opportunity to sit and chat to Sensei Benny, I always take something away from it. He's very philosophical and faith based. Most of all, he's what I call, 'a doer'. He doesn't just talk, he does. He is such an inspiration as a teacher and a warrior of our arts. Anyway, getting back to 'Force Five', I remember being at the audition in front of the 'Enter The Dragon' director, Bob Clouse and ETD Producer, Fred Weintraub and thinking to myself, 'What chance have I got? I am competing against some of the top martial artists in the country and I have a funny accent to boot. Yet at the end of the day, it got down to the final ten people, and I was one of them. That was a huge shift in attitude for me, because I realised, I had trained just as hard as anyone there and had the necessary skills. I then immediately changed my attitude and adopted the mindset from, 'Why me, to Why Not Me?

RB: You were given a chance because you worked hard and deserved it. You can thank people for giving you opportunities, but you've also got to recognise the role of your own character and abilities in seizing them.

RN: I believe we can absolutely create our own luck. Chuck of course was special because of everything he did for me in the beginning and was very instrumental in presenting me with opportunities, but as I often say to students looking for advice, 'Do not take yourself out of the equation'. Yes, certain people in your life can give you opportunities and all that, but if you don't have what it takes and aren't willing to put in all the hard work, you will never last.

RB: When I met Chuck, he was a really nice person.

RN: Oh yeah, and he trained as hard as anyone. I remember I took Cynthia to one of our morning training sessions at his house and it nearly killed her. She was so impressed with how long and how hard we trained in those early sessions.

RB: What prompted you to go to Hong Kong?

RN: That came about through Pat Johnson, who I mentioned earlier, working with Jackie Chan on The Big Brawl. He recommended me to Jackie as someone who would make a good baddie in one of his movies. So, I was in Japan with Linda Ronstadt when I received a phone call from an Asian lady who said, 'Jackie wants you to come and work on a movie. What's your price?' I asked, 'When would he need me there?' She replied, 'In three days.' I said that I couldn't – I was on tour doing bodyguard work! And that was that! A short time later, though, they contacted me again and offered me some work on Twinkle Twinkle Lucky Stars.

RB: Did you know what to expect doing a Hong Kong movie?

RN: (laughs) Not in the slightest as it turns out! I was on the plane, thinking that I'd be able to do a little bit of this and that and basically have a good time. So, I was there initially for about three weeks and did bugger all. I was originally meant to do the main fight scene with Jackie, but he'd unfortunately injured his shoulder on another shoot around he was shooting at the same time. That's why I ended up doing that main fight with Sammo Hung. We shot that fight, seven days a week, for three and a half weeks straight, 18 hours a day. For the first three days, I remember I was getting quite frustrated, due to the different emphases on timing and power that I was used to in Western shoots. The legendary Japanese actor, Yasuaki Kurata – who by the wat, was so helpful and such a gentleman – saw this and pulled me aside for some advice. I'm paraphrasing, but he said, 'If you really

want to do more of these movies here in Hong Kong, don't say anything. Just do it. The Hong Kong stuntie,s pretty much don't really care what you want to do. It's their movie set. So just do it as many times as you are asked and take all the bumps until they get the take they liked.' I took that advice and pretty much credit that as to why I got asked back numerous times to work with them. I do recall though, going back to my hotel room and saying out loud to myself: 'If I can get through this, I can get through anything!'

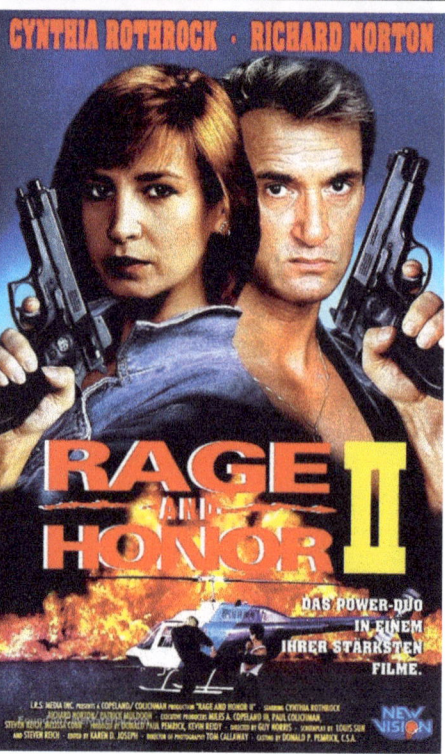

Sammo was a powerhouse, especially then. The way he delivered his punches and kicks was as close to full contact as you can get on a movie set.

RB: Mark Houghton told me that Sammo doesn't pull his punches.

RN: He's very tough. Even on a film set, you can pretty much tell if someone can really fight and Sammo got my respect, right from the get-go. Especially his spinning back kick. Man, he can really plant that thing. I remember I got hit with bare-fisted uppercuts under the chin. They put my face in front of a camera for insert shots and Sammo just punched me. That's not fake! Of course, he wasn't doing it as fast as he can, but it was still bare knuckles. I found a little bit of cotton wool to put in my teeth because I didn't want to chip them. And that sidekick when he hits me with it and drives me back against the wall? We did that about thirty times. I think he started across the other side of the street, and I just got planted! (Laughs).

RB: How did he treat you overall?

RN: Gratefully, I got on well with Sammo. For whatever reasons, I had the timing that well suited Sammo and Jackie's choreography, so he liked that. Also, following Kurata's advice, I didn't complain at all about getting hit, which I know gained the HK stunt teams respect. I trained very hard back then and was used to hard contact when it came to fight training. He could basically kick the crap out of me, and I was okay with it. I do remember jokingly saying one day, 'Ok, but as long as I can hit you back just as hard!' The thing I respected is that he WANTED you to hit him back just as hard! Also, his athleticism was extraordinary.

RB: Who did the choreography?

RN: In this fight, this was pretty much one hundred percent Sammo. Jackie was kind of peripheral to the scene. He did ask me what I felt were my favourite techniques, which I appreciated, so I told him and he worked with that input and included facets of my fighting style in the choreography. He seemed to really like me. I didn't get any of the grief that some people unfortunately got from the stunt team. Sammo took me to editing a lot of nights and Jackie was taking me shopping all over Hong Kong

for cameras and such. I hung out with him a lot. I had dinner at numerous times with them both. So suddenly, I guess I was in the 'inner circle', and I feel the stunt team saw this and left me alone as this made me okay! There's a scene where I get hauled off a bike and Jackie chases me. One of the stunt team was telling me that I had to do it a certain way and suddenly Jackie intervened and said, 'He knows. He knows what to do.' I tell you what, though, I learnt so bloody much. Sammo taught me many tricks of theirs, things like what he called a three-point punch and how to make it work for camera. It looked strange to me at the time but worked beautifully on film. I learnt a lot of things about shooting an action scene, Hong Kong style.

RB: Why did you not use weapons?

RN: They had no idea I could use weapons, and they didn't ever ask me! The one time I did use weapons was in 'Magic Crystal', with Andy Lau and Cynthia. Wong Jing asked and when I told him I could use the 'Sai', they incorporated into one of the big fights and it was terrific result.

RB. Are there big differences in shooting a Hong Kong movie to a Western action movie?

There's a huge difference between the American and Hong Kong styles. The shooting in Hong Kong was very organic. We filmed a section, and they often had no idea where it was going to go. It's why it took so long. Sammo would look at the edit each night and decide which direction he wanted the fight to go and how much longer he wanted it to be. They pretty much went by their gut, which meant they were never 'locked' into a master of a fight scene, but allowed it to develop spontaneously, which I feel is pretty cool, if not time consuming. Everything I did was mostly rehearsed in front of the camera. That's why it took 20, sometimes 30, takes to reach the level of excellence that Sammo or Jackie wanted.

RB: Jackie often did that. In other films, you're on a schedule and must get things done in a certain time. I guess working with Jackie and Sammo, you would have take after take until they felt it was right.

RN: Well, It's their baby and their movie. They knew they had control. Jackie once laughed telling me how he'd done something like 330 takes on one little piece of choreography on an action scene.

RB: I think the record is over 1000 takes on the shuttlecock scene in The Dragon Lord.

RN: They both knew they had complete control of the shoot and schedule. I got a little frustrated sometimes. I'd find myself standing by the monitor, watching, and wondering what they were looking for in each take. I often couldn't see much difference from take to take. Then you'd get to take 18 or 20 and Sammo would suddenly say, 'Ok, we move on, and there was always that little bit of magic in what he chose. He obviously always had an element he was looking for and was not happy until he got it and it contained that level of excellence he always went after. That fight scene I did with Jackie on City Hunter took six and a half bloody weeks to film. I used to do whole movies in that amount of time. (Laughs). It was simply exhausting! Remember, there were no unions in Hong Kong back then and the stunties were paid a small monthly retainer, so budget wise, relative to a western shoot, they could go virtually go on filming forever.!

RB: Did you get to go to the premiere?

RN: No, I always went back home afterwards. I can't even remember how I got to see 'Twinkle Twinkle Lucky Stars'. I remember that I saw City Hunter for the first time in Los Angeles, probably at the film market. It cracked me up! Because I didn't see everything they filmed at the time, it was so funny seeing the rest of the movie for the first time. It was a big kick playing a bad guy back then in those movies. For instance, I would do an evil laugh and under play it and Sammo would stop me and tell me to do it much more extravagantly. Everything was so over the top. That was the era. I understood very early in the game that if you didn't jump on board the 'fun' part of what they did, you just simply didn't belong in those movies. You were almost a caricature and that is what made those early movies so much fun, along with the tongue in cheek action. You had to accept that it was larger than life and go for the ride, or just don't put your hand up in the first place.

RB: I've got to ask. That catchphrase – painful – whose idea was that?

RN: I'm not one hundred percent sure! I think it was Sammo. It's got to have been.

When I spoke in English in those movies, I'd say something at the approximate length of whatever they were going to dub over in Mandarin. It became a running gag!

RB: Even people who genuinely can't remember much about any films they watch remember that catchphrase. I've seen people say it when they're messing about fighting.

RN: That's very funny! You know, people often ask me what was it like to first be offered to work with Jackie Chan and how much fun it must have been? I tell them the truth – yes, it was great, but it wasn't always fun. It was bloody hard work. Also, at the time it was just a gig. Because I wasn't particularly a follower of Hong Kong cinema, I wasn't going there already over-awed by working with Jackie and Sammo, because I didn't really know a lot about either of them. Of course, after the fact, I became a huge fan and consider them the absolute maestros of action cinema. It's particularly thirty years later that I realise how incredibly privileged I was to work on some of those iconic 1980s Hong Kong films.

RB: Did they offer you any more roles?

RN: Yes. I did several movies there after 'Twinkle, Twinkle. Sammo said that he wanted to work with me again on Millionaires Express and I also did 'Magic Crystal' with Andy Lau and Cynthia. Back then, I was also touring a lot with various Rock'n'roll bands and doing other movies in places like Los Angeles and the Philippines. It was a great time for low budget films.

RB: I guess it's the highest accolade to be called back because they rarely did it.

RN: Of course, I was absolutely thrilled. Sammo then offered me the main bad guy role in Mr Nice Guy, which was so cool as it was being shot in Melbourne, Australia. By then I had the utmost respect for Sammo as a filmmaker, and the thought of working in Melbourne and filming a movie with him was a fantastic opportunity for me.

RB: Did you hang out?

RN: Yeah, he'd invite me out to Chinese restaurants and places. I remember one day we were sitting in a Chinese restaurant, and he suddenly remarked that he'd seen a lot of my movies. Of course, that in itself floored and somewhat embarrassed me. He then went on to say that he very much liked my performances, but that the problem with my acting for him, was that I was 'too normal'. I asked him what he meant by that. He then went on to give me examples of performances by people like Gary Oldman and Mel Gibson in 'Lethal Weapon', when he behaved like one of the Three Stooges, where they might have seemed over the top in some scenes, but people certainly remembered them. No one remembers 'normal', he said, emphatically. I remember thinking, 'Wow, that's surprisingly good advice from a dramatic point of view and not what I expected.' I never forgot that bit of wisdom from the legendary Sammo Hung.

RB: If you talk to people who've watched Sammo films, you can see that he played up to that element. Although, I think he was on a learning curve.

RN: I watched 'My Beloved Bodyguard' and his acting was so powerful. No exaggeration, no wide eyes. That's 180 degrees from the Sammo I worked with in the 1980s. He was forever on a learning curve of improvement and innovation. I

mean how could you not be, when you look at the volume of films Sammo has Directed and acted in to this date. And he is still going strong. Much respect.

RB: You can go back to First Mission to see him take a role and play it completely straight. He's a proper actor. Look at him in Martial Law.

RN: Absolutely. And you can see Jackie do that in The Karate Kid. You see people like Margot Robbie and Scarlett Johansson, and the level of excellence they expect from themselves is why they have the careers they have. It's the same with Jackie and Sammo. They constantly look to evolve and improve. Look at that fight between Donnie Yen and Sammo Hung in SPL. Mixed martial arts – how good was that? The movement and energy – that's why Sammo's the best.

RB: If someone said to me, who's the best fight choreographer, I'd say Sammo Hung.

RN: I'm totally with you. There's nobody I respect more to this day as a director, choreographer and performer in action cinema. I've always said that he could do a fight scene of any style, with anything. Look at the little Judo scene with Michelle Yeoh. He could completely mix it up. Hats off to him. I wish in Mr Nice Guy that we'd done a big final fight between me and Jackie, but the budget went way over and we basically ran out of time. I mean wasn't even there when 'Giancarlo' got hit with the huge mining truck! I remember saying to Sammo, 'There's no point using me if you're not going to have a climactic fight in the end between me and Jackie!' Anyway, It didn't happen, but I wish it had, because I'd have loved to have seen what they came up with at that point and been a part of their evolution in fight sequences with me.

RB: What was it like working on Millionaires Express?

RN: It was incredibly hard work. I had a fight with Kurata San, which was fantastic, and Yukari Oshima, which was fantastic too. I was quite comfortable because I was walking into familiar territory with Sammo and his team. I was totally mentally prepared for the ride. The cast is a Who's Who of quality, so I had an amazingly good time. I got to learn a little more about the famous Peking Opera school, because there was one guy from there who doubled for Kurata-san and he was taking some wrecks. Man, he took some hard bumps. I made a comment about that, and I was told about their incredibly rigorous and sometimes brutal training. The hardest part for me was injuring one of my knees before the shoot. I'd done a film in the Philippines where I'd cut my knees in a quarry doing some action stuff. I went to Hong Kong, and when I started to do the fight scenes, my knee suddenly started to swell up. It turned out I could hardly pull a boot on. At the beginning of the fight, they wanted me to kick Kurata in the head, and I nearly fainted when he forearm blocked my kick. They took my boot off and found that it was full of blood and pus, as I has a serious staph infection. So I had to do the fight in between trips to the hospital to have it drained and treated with antibiotics.

RB: When was the last time you saw Sammo?

RN: Not since Mr Nice Guy. I'd dearly love to see him again, though, if only for old time sake. It's sad to hear about his apparent health issues.
Thinking back to Twinkle Twinkle, I remember talking through a fight scene with him, where he's going on about doing flips and somersaults off a table, and I was literally looking around for the stunt double. I was thinking, there's no way this guy's going to be able to do that. And, of course, he did it himself over twenty times. I knew then that there was so much more to this man than meets the eye. Jackie once said that Sammo was built like an elephant but moved like a monkey, which in Chinese terms was a huge compliment If I got to work with him again, it would be like coming 'full circle' for me in my career in action films.

RB: How would you sum Sammo up?

RN: I got to see many facets of him over the years. The Sammo that absolutely made his stunt guys tremble. I watched him do that fight scene with Kurata's double in 'Twinkle, Twinkle', where he hit him over and over with tennis rackets. Afterwards, I noticed the stuntie lying in the corner, contorted with pain. Sammo just beat the absolute snot out of him. I remember on Millionaires Express he shin-kicks this stunt guy in the neck in a scene. There were three of them by the time we got the shot. He hit them so hard, that they were literally out cold. They'd drag them out by the ankles and the next guy would come in and get hit. He once took me to watch a shoot he was directing whilst in Hong Kong and they had a stunt where this guy would come flying out of the second floor window of a restaurant, bounce on the canopy of the first floor, then off and onto the roof of a car that's driving in. No pads on the road. I mean how do you even time that? So I go upstairs and there was a stuntie lying on the ground and he had both legs strapped with sticks. He'd tried the stunt and missed the canopy and car, and broke both his legs. They were setting up another guy to try. Sammo said 'Action' and the guy performed the stunt. I turned to Sammo and said, 'Wow, congratulations, you've got it!' Sammo had an angry look on his face and started screaming at the stunt team. I asked Sammo what he'd said, and he told me that he'd told them to do it again because he wanted the stunt guy to bounce faster off the canopy. I remember I laughed and said to him, 'You guys are insane!' So, I saw that side to Sammo. But I also saw the caring and brilliant side. Someone who would never accept mediocrity in his pursuit of excellence as he saw it. In Twinkle, Twinkle and other films we worked in together, he sometimes got a stunt guy to take a really bad kick or dangerous bump instead of me, the Gwailo, or outsider. So I feel he always had concerns and took care of me. He gave me that great acting advice. He took me to editing. He took me to restaurants. He took delight in our friendship. Yes, he's a tough guy, but also an incredibly thoughtful and humorous guy. I feel I was fortunate enough and saw all sides of this man, especially his lifelong passion for what he does. He truly is one of the most talented people in action cinema I have ever had the pleasure of working with. Total respect.

RB Thank you Richard for the great Interview.

SAMMO HUNG
UNSEEN OR unmade
By Big Mike Leeder

You can't miss the importance of Sammo Hung to Hong Kong Action Cinema both in front and behind the camera, he's an Actor, a Director, an Action Choreographer, a Producer, a Writer and so much more. He's discovered new talent, he's reinvented established talent both in front and behind the camera over the years, and while he's now slowed down a little celebrating his 70th Birthday this year, the man still has a full dance card. Now while we know the movies Sammo has made, lets have a look at some of the films that could have been….

Winners and Sinners 2: Sammo's Boogaloo

While everyone accepts Winners and Sinners, My Lucky Stars and Twinkle Twinkle Lucky Stars to be parts of the same franchise, the Winners and Sinners team not only popped up in a cameo in the Sammo produced POM POM starring Richard Ng and John Sham (Ng already being a member of the established Winners/Lucky Stars team and Sham appearing in Twinkle Twinkle Lucky Stars as Rosamund Kwan's flatmate who ends up joining the action), but there was set to be an official Winners and Sinners 2 and shooting did begin on the film, only for Sammo to abandon the footage and reboot the concept into the bigger budget My Lucky Stars.

During Sammo's tenure at Golden Harvest several of his projects would hit a bump or two in the road, from Spooky Spooky a supernatural action comedy starring Alfred Cheung, Anthony Chan, Wu Ma and Joyce Godenzi, shooting for which went on hiatus while Sammo reteamed with Jackie Chan and Yuen Biao for Dragons Forever, and would resume with a total overhaul when Sammo learnt that at least two directors had screened his footage and borrowed ideas for their own movies!

Sammo was also a Producer on Demon Hunters, an English language adaptation of Mr Vampire which began shooting with Jack Scalia from Pointman, Michelle Phillips replacing the originally announced Tanya Roberts and Yuen Wah who had played the vampire in Mr Vampire, now inheriting the Vampire buster role originated by Lam Ching-ying. Shooting began but imploded after only a few days of shooting, and the footage was tucked away and Sammo and Producer David Chan to this day refuse to talk about what went wrong.

Sammo Hung's TEKKEN and the AVENGING FIST

The year 2000 saw Sammo in demand as an actor, action director and director following

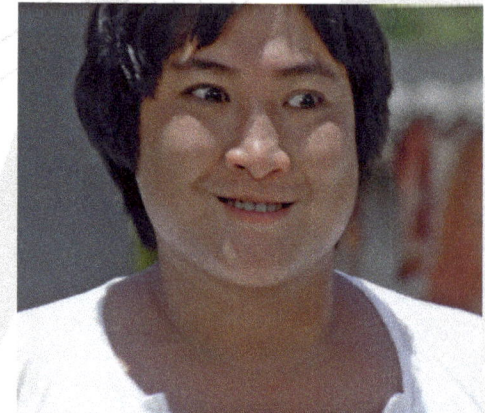

his return to Hong Kong after two seasons of Martial Law, his first project in China/Hong Kong following Martial Law was a show that almost seemed like the 3rd Season of Martial Law as Sammo played a senior Cop assigned to a special crime busting unit that includes his youngest son Sammy Hung and a young Fan Bing-bing. According to Sammo however they were very different, "Martial Law, I am a Chinese Cop who goes to America! In this series I am an American Cop who comes to China!"

In the midst of this, Sammo was in talks to be both Action Choreographer and Director for a live action adaptation of the video game Tekken, with Namco and Sammo having several meetings to discuss the project in Hong Kong and Japan.

The project ended up falling through, in part when Sammo was hired for a project entitled The Avenging Fist, by Director Andrew Lau and Wong Jing which was shall we say a grey area unlicensed adaptation of Tekken itself, with Sammo playing the older version of the character plated by Ekin Cheng, and rocking a cool trench coat, fedora and oh yes the POWER GLOVE from Tekken. There had been a similar situation when Jackie Chan and Golden Harvest had licensed characters from the Streetfighter 2 game for use in City Hunter, and Wong Jing who directed City Hunter then went ahead and made Future Cops, which is very much his take on Streetfighter with all the grey area characters and likeness's you could imagine!

NOTE: Tekken would eventually hit the screen with Rapid Fire director Dwight H Little at the helm and a cast that includes Jon Foo (Rush Hour the TV series) Cary Tagawa (Mortal Kombat), and Gary Daniels as Bryan Fury. It would eventually be followed by a prequel Tekken 2: Kazuya's Revenge starring Kane Kosugi with cameo appearances by both Gary Daniels and Cary Tagawa, while Brahim Chab (Boyka: Undisputed, Vanguard) provided fight choreography.

Sammo Hung: Soul Calibre

Sammo then teamed with Producer Noel E Vega who he had worked with Martial Law, and began developing with Namco an official Soul Calibre movie, with a proposed US$50 million budget which would have seen Sammo bringing his style of action to the sword play fantasy game. Unfortunately despite a couple of years development, the project fell into development hell where it lives to this day!

Sammo Hung: Time's Up!

Announced as part of a slate of projects for Producer Takkie Yeung, Time's Up was a cross between Die Hard with a Vengeance and 24, as a terrorist rages war on the innocent and the fate of the world lies in the hands of a gun toting high kicking kung fu monk played by Sammo Hung. The film was pre-sold at the Hong Kong Filmart in 2001, and initial casting began but following the events of 9-11, the project was pushed back and then faded into the darkness of what could have been.

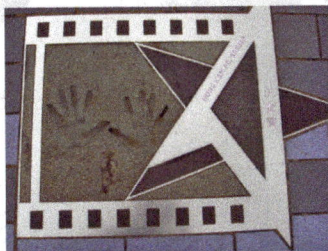

Sammo De Bergerac: Sammo to play Cyrano

During the shooting of what would eventually become The Medallion, Sammo spoke about adapting Edmond Rostand's 1897 verse play Cyrano De Bergerac to the screen as a Chnese language adaptation. The original version tells of Hercule Savinen de Cyrano De Bergerac a Nobleman who serves in the French Army. He's a brash, strong man of many talents, he;s a remarkable fighter, a gifted poet and a musician however he is gifted with an overabundance of nose, which causes him to doubt himself, and he has convinced himself that no woman could ever love him.

This stops him from openly expressing his feelings for the beautiful Roxanne, to the point of finding himself helping the handsome if dim witted Christian to begin to romance her, with him providing the words of love which win her heart.

Its been adapted for the stage and screen numerous times, with Jose Ferrer's version nd the late 80's Steve Martin adaptation Roxanne probably being two of the best known. If you've seen Sammo's performance in 8 Taels of Gold, or the way he woos Deanie Yip in both Dragons Forever and The Owl Vs Bumbo, you know Sammo could carry this off, with Sammo swapping out the nasal issue with that of his shall we say size, stop laughing at the back Rick! Sammo has spoken about the project at various times, the last time we spoke about it was on Rise of the Legend when he mentioned it as something he was still interested in, but sadly until now its not made any raal progress. The release of the recent Peter Dinklage take on Cyranno brought the idea of Sammo's take on the

story flashing back to me.

Obi-Hung? Now that's a name I haven't heard in a very long time!

SAMMO HUNG: THE STAR WARS CONNECTION

A long, long time ago in a Galaxy Far Away, we very nearly got to see Sammo do a jump spinning back kick to Jar Jar Binks, if only! But seriously, not once but twice we very nearly had Sammo Hung joining the Star Wars universe both in front and behind the camera. Sadly, the force wasn't with us and that didn't happen but lets talk about what could have been. Star Wars: The Phantom Menace had been a huge commercial success, lets not talk about the critical response, Director and Creator George Lucas wanted to up the ante with the second prequel and one of the ways he was thinking about changing things

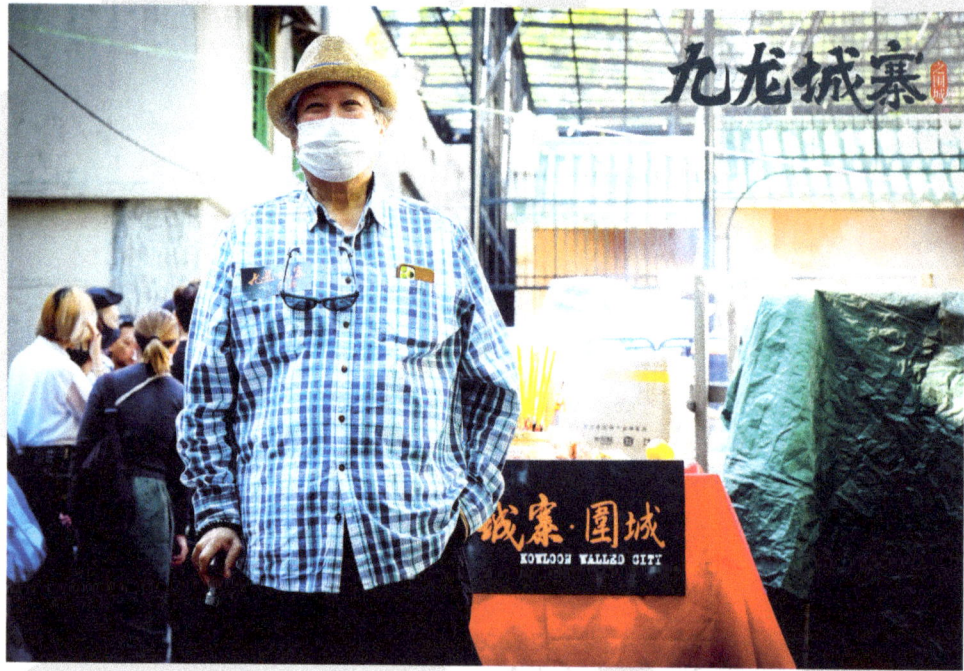

up was in terms of action, and Lucasfilm did reach out to Sammo Hung about the possibility of joining the franchise as fight choreographer. Now imagine what Sammo could have done with the action scenes in Episode 2 or any Star Wars movie? Sammo styled lightsabre play as the Jedi battle Jango Fett and imagine a Sammo styled take on Yoda Vs Count Dooku. Sadly after initial discussion, nothing moved forward and instead of Sammo choreographing Jedi Knights, we got him choreographing Gwyneth Paltrow in View From the Top!

And some years later with the release of Gareth Edwards ROGUE ONE: A STAR WARS STORY, we got Donnie Yen in fine form as Chirrut Imwe, but he was very nearly partnered by Sammo Hung rather than Jiang Wen as Baze Malbus. Jiang Wen did a great job as the laconic Baze, but the 'weight' Sammo could have brought to the character would have been incredible, but my only worry would be would the double team of Donnie and Sammo be given enough to do in the film? Donnie gets a few nice moments, but would they have been able to give Sammo enough to do, or would it have been a waste of his talents as with the waste of Iko Uwais, Cecep and Yayan in Star Wars: The Force Awakens, its great to see them but they don't get to do anything!

RETURN OF THE LUCKY STARS

Frustratingly, not only did Sammo decide to revisit the LUCKY STARS franchise (Winners & Sinners, My Lucky Stars, Twinkle Lucky Stars, plus Lucky Stars Go Places, How to Meet the Lucky Stars and Ghost Punting), with Dennis Chan (Kickboxer) writing and co-producing, and many of the original Lucky Stars cast including Eric Tsang and Richard Ng coming back for cameos, and Yuen Wah (Eastern Condors), Yuen Qiu (Kung Fu Hustle), Tony Leung (Island of Fire), Danny Lee (City on Fire), Chin Siu-ho (Mr Vampire) and Eddie Peng (Rise of the Legend) joining the cast but shooting had begun in China with several action sequences including a tourist coach ending up white water rafting, a brutal streetfight and car chase already shot before budgetary issues affected production causing it to be put on hold, and sadly as till now, never having resumed.

Note: There is another movie called Return of the Lucky Stars featuring the majority of the Lucky Stars team Richard Ng, Eric Tsang etc but doesn't feature or have any involvement from Sammo, so lets call it non cannon.

Sammo Hung: The Medal of the Dawn

Sammo was set to helm his own Wolf

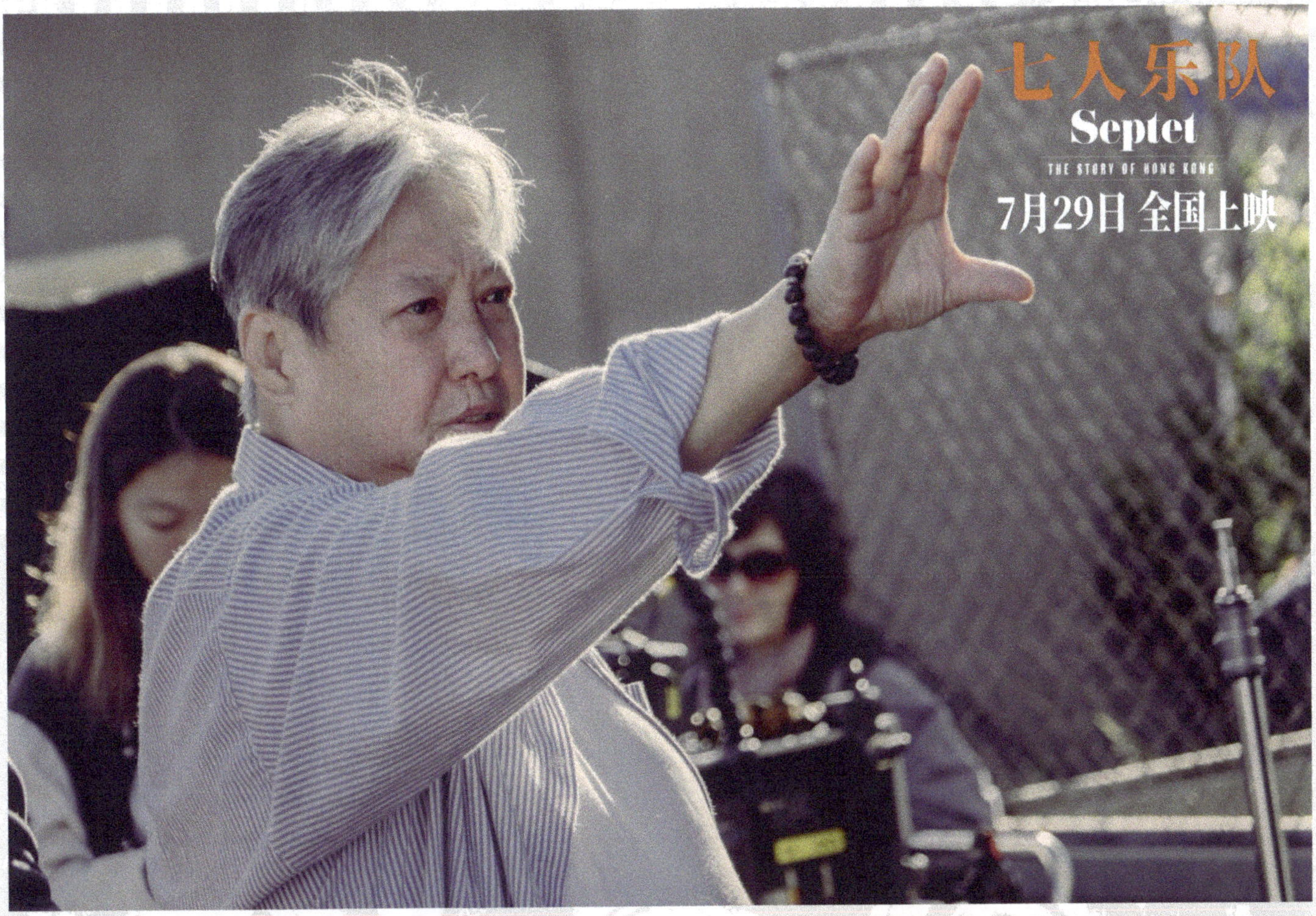
七人乐队
Septet
THE STORY OF HONG KONG
7月29日 全国上映

边缘行者
MAN ON THE EDGE
洪 金 宝
嚣张卧底 背水一搏
4.15
嚣张开战
黄 明 升

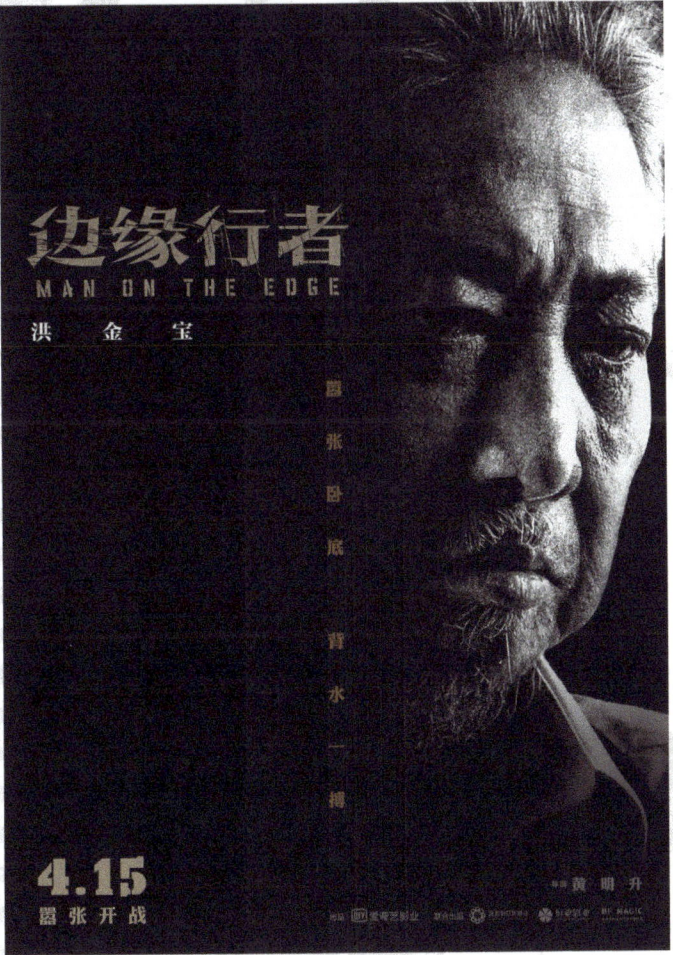

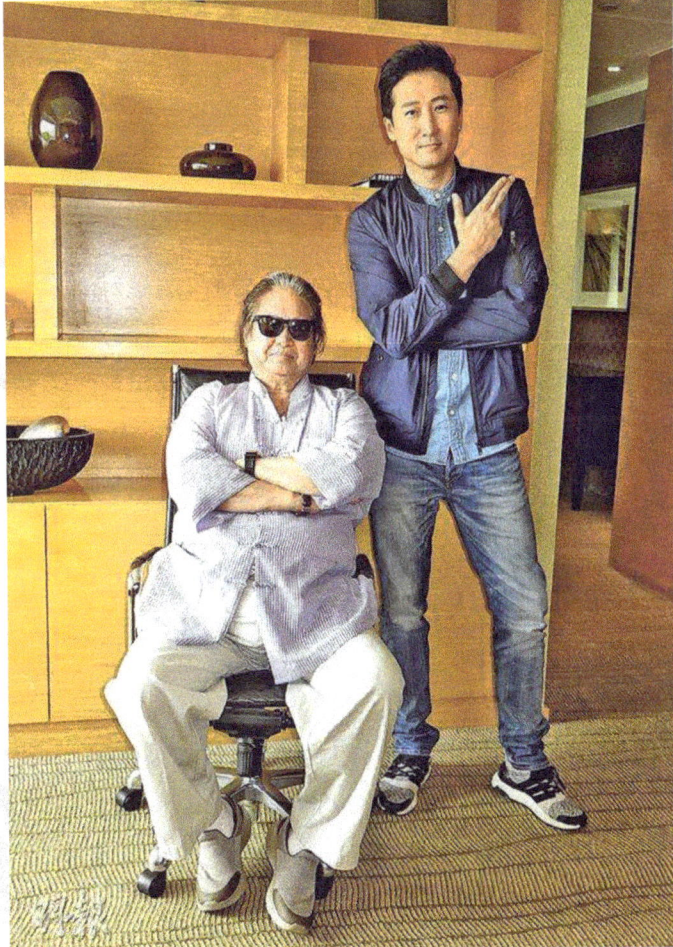

Warrior styled military action movie The Medal of the Dawn, starring Nick Cheung (Nightfall) and Janice Man from Helios, along with the Sik Seal-lung the now grown up Jet Li junior from the Shaolin Popeye series of movies. The film which would have been Sammo's first military themed movie since Eastern Condors, had completed Pre-Production and was days away from starting shooting when Covid-19 shut down the majority of the world, and they are still trying to reschedule the cast so the film can still be made.

Sammo's most recent Big Screen appearance was in Man on the Edge a Triad drama directed by Sam Wong (Police Story 3: Supercop) alongside Alex Fong, Simon Yam, and Ritchie Ren, and he'll
soon be back on the big screen, behind the camera helming one of the chapters of the highly anticipated SEPTEP: THE STORY OF HONG KONG which features short stories by Sammo, Yuen Woo-ping, Ann Hui, Patrick Tam, Johnnie To, Tsui Hark and the late Ringo Lam. Hung's story sees his eldest son Timmy playing a Peking Opera Teacher, while second son Jimmy worked behind the scenes on this one.

And we'll see him on screen again in full fighting form in City of Darkness aka Kowloon Walled City, Directed by Johnathan Li with Soi Cheang Producing, and Kenji Tanigaki (Rurouni Kenshin series, Snake Eyes) as action director. Hung stars alongside Ritchie Ren, Louis Koo and Philip Ng (Once Upon a Time in Shanghai)

Page 23   Eastern Heroes Sammo Hung Special

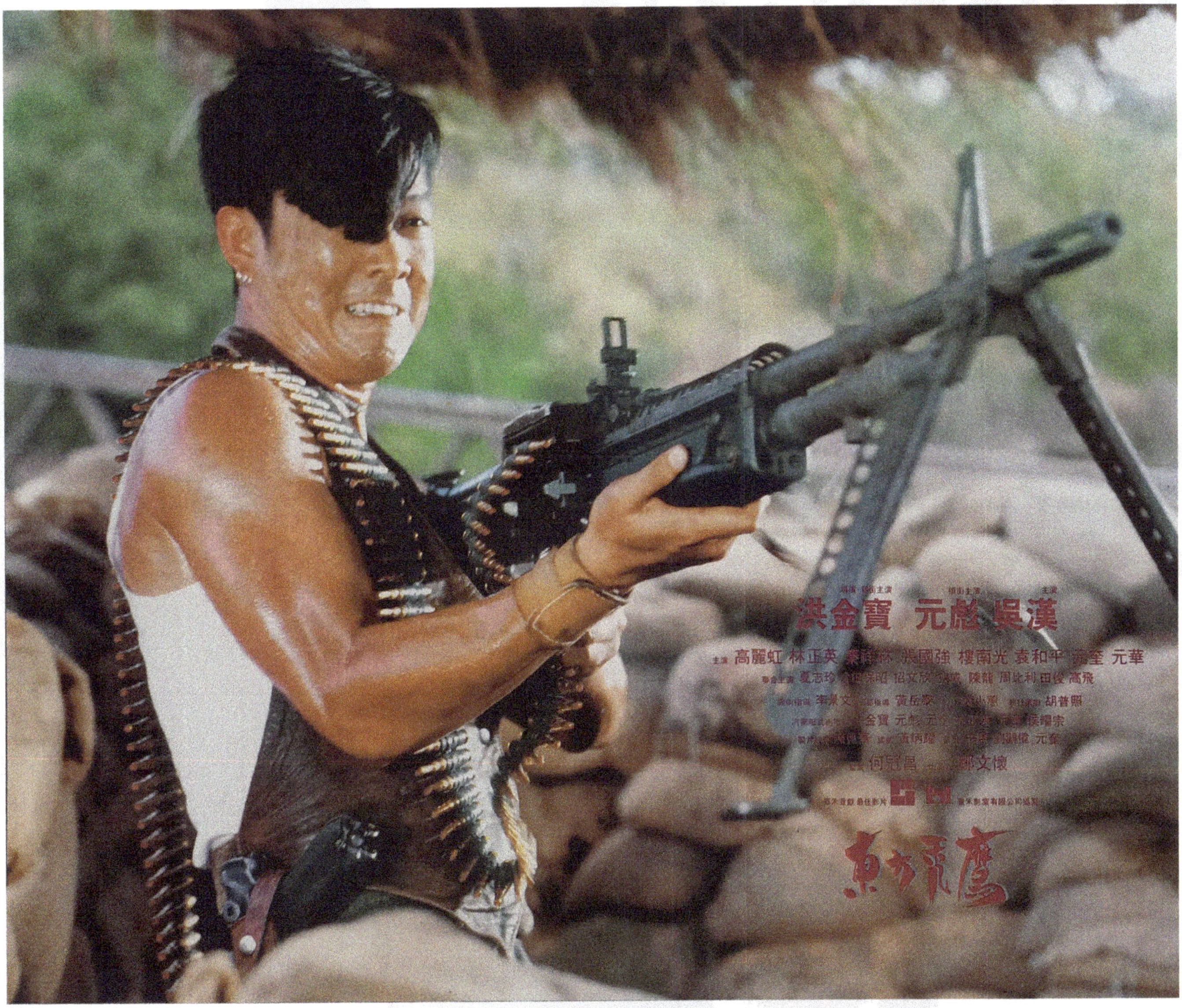
洪金寶 元彪 吳漢
高麗虹 林正英 張國強 樓南光 袁和平 元華
陳龍 周比利 田俊 高飛
胡普照
何冠昌 鄒文懷
東方禿鷹

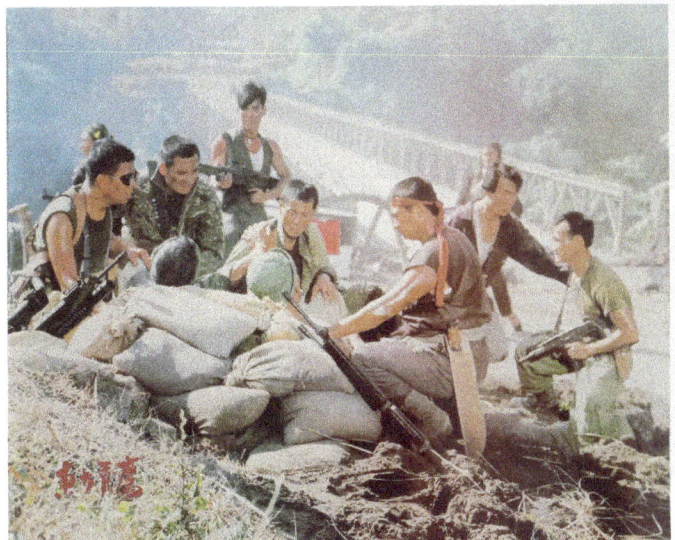

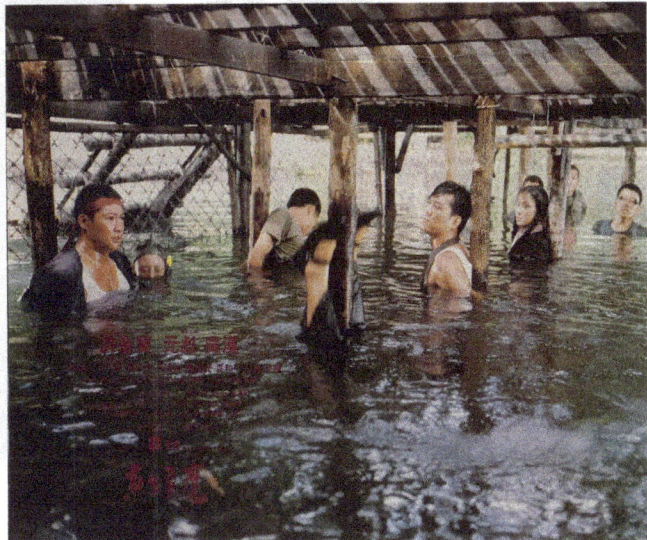

How Sammo Hung inspired an autistic girl to become...

FATTY KARATE

瘦虎肥龍

By Harriet Connor

Growing up, I was never the most athletic child. I had tried a number of different sports, including gymnastics, badminton and swimming, but none were for me. I did learn how to swim, but it's never something I did competitively. I was far more into my arts, excelling at reading, writing and music. As a youngster, reading was my favorite activity and Enid Blyton was one of my favorite authors. I had wanted to write when I grew up, but unfortunately I still haven't written a full book. Maybe one day I'll do it.

On the other hand, my parents have always been athletic - my mother is into horse riding and running, and as a child she had tried desperately to get me and my younger sister into horse riding. That was also never to be, sadly, as when my pony I'd had since

birth died when I reached the age of twelve I effectively gave up. Since that happened, I have only ridden a small handful of times, the most recent being at a session organised by my local Riding for the Disabled school. Horse riding was something that was an absolute novelty as a youngster, but not a hobby I would personally ever take up again.

My autism diagnosis, which I received at the age of 16, came as a shock to absolutely nobody. I had suspected there was something not quite right about me after making friends with an autistic boy at my school when I was 14 and recognising some similarities in our behavior's. It took two years for mc to be referred to a child psychologist, who conducted my diagnosis within a few months or so of the referral.

After pursuing a 4 year long degree in Literature and successfully graduating from university at the age of 22, I was kind of stuck in limbo. My life wasn't really going in any sort of linear direction, and was trying to make new friends, having moved to a new town 2 years prior. Socialising wasn't really something I was interested in, so I didn't bother attending any local clubs or activities, choosing instead to befriend people over the internet (which, I will admit, has been both a bane and a boon). I felt like I wouldn't be welcomed at any activities or clubs, since I was this new weird kid from outside of town with a disability to boot. Since I wasn't really doing any sports or physical activity, unfortunately I ended up slightly on the chubby side.

One day for some reason I decided to look up clips from Jackie Chan Adventures on

YouTube, most likely for the nostalgia factor. In the "Recommended for You" section, there were a few clips from some of Jackie's older movies, one of which was Project

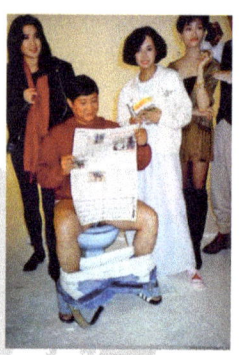

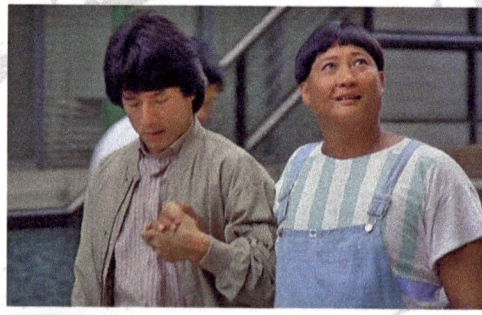
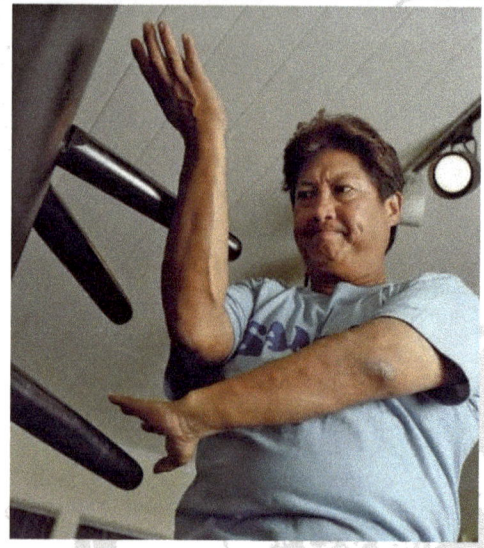
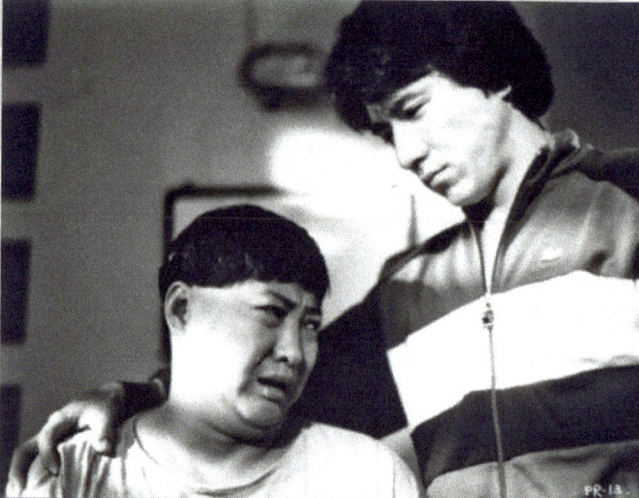

A. After watching said clip and enjoying it, I then went looking for the full movie, and found it on YouTube. For the next 1 hour and 45 minutes, I sat, mesmerised, as Jackie Chan and his friends battled their foes with their fists. Out of all the actors in the movie, one stood out to me the most. A chubby guy with a sleek, black bob cut and a cheeky grin. Any time this man appeared on screen, I was in awe of his fighting ability. "Who is he?" I wondered out loud, before looking up the cast list for the movie and finding out that his name was Sammo Hung. Browsing more of his filmography online, I was absolutely stunned by what I saw. Here was a man, built similar to myself, who was a phenomenal fighter, with many martial arts and movie stunt credits to his name. During my research into this man's back catalogue, one movie of Sammo Hung's really spoke to me and stuck out to me, and that was "Heart of Dragon". The credits reel of that movie (from the Japanese release) had actually come up in a playlist of Jackie Chan film clips I had been watching, and the title of the video was in Japanese. After copy and pasting the title of the video into Google I was only really able to find multiple YouTube uploads of the song Tokyo Saturday Night and nothing else. However, after searching for the song in English, I was able to find the movie, much to my delight.

A quote on the Wikipedia article for that movie jumped out at me and made me stop in my tracks. The quote in question, from an interview Sammo Hung did (which I later found out was included on a DVD release of the movie) stated that he had apparently been asked to perform stunts for the movie (as was typical of other movies he starred in during the 1980s) however he had refused, replying to the interviewer that "My character was mentally retarded, mentally disabled, so how can you ask me to fall down and suddenly become well again? And fight? They knew my fighting skills and wanted me to be part of the action but I thought that would have completely destroyed the tone of the film, the principles behind the film.". This, as an autistic person, confused me. Surely disabled people were like any other type of people, and should be given the opportunity to do martial arts too? I probably completely misinterpreted his comments, which is common in autistic people, however at that time, I was determined to prove that disabled people could do martial arts (a later Google search on disability in martial arts showed people with Down's Syndrome and physical disabilities doing karate kata and taekwondo forms, so I most likely did take Sammo's comment the wrong way). I now feel I need to point out that I meant no malice in my actions, as stated earlier I missed the point and took what was said to heart.

Deciding there and then that I wanted to do a martial art or similar activity, I immediately fired off an email to a local autism support service I had previously used.
Do you know of any local martial arts clubs that would take on autistic adults? I asked the support staff in my email, hoping they might actually know of someone that did.
They replied a few hours later confirming that they knew of a karate club locally that had taken on autistic adults in the past.
Here's the sensei's name and phone number, they replied.
I started training in Shotokan karate back in January 2019, I was so excited to start training, because I wanted to be as good as Sammo and Jackie one day (despite the fact that I also knew that would take an awful lot of work and time, as well as the fact that they had both trained since childhood). For my first lesson, my mother came with me and spoke to the sensei, telling him I was autistic and that I would try my best in the class, as I was not usually a sporty person so me wanting to take up a martial art had come completely out of the blue. When she returned, she was surprised to find that I had

enjoyed myself and really wanted to return the next week. I remember the journey home after my first class, with my mum driving, eager to know how I had got on at my first lesson, and me, excitedly telling her what I had learned and what the sensei was like.

Karate has changed my life for the better through karate, I have gained confidence, self-respect and a very good friend, who like me is also autistic and into a lot of the same stuff as me (which is why we befriended each other in the first place). My physical health has also improved and I am slowly becoming more flexible due to all the stretching and kicking involved.

My nickname, "Fatty Karate" was chosen in honor of Sammo Hung. One of his many names is "Fat Dragon" (after one of his earlier movies, Enter the Fat Dragon). I thought to myself that if Sammo can be Fat Dragon, then I can be Fatty Karate. The name just stuck, and it's pretty much now one of the only nicknames I go by (although very few people call me that in real life, probably because they find it embarrassing).

In my honest opinion, I believe martial arts are for everyone. As I have mentioned earlier in this article, I have an Autism Spectrum Disorder, and believed I might not fit in at karate due to me being very different from the other students (for example, I carry my kit in a backpack adorned with LEGO Ninjago keyrings). For some strange reason, I also believed that you had to have a certain body type to be able to do martial arts - that you had to be tall and skinny, and possibly also a runner, as I knew martial artists had to move fast. Although build and athletic ability does play a part in a person's ability to perform properly in martial arts, it's not the MOST important thing. The most important thing (well certainly in my opinion, anyway) is actually a person's mentality towards the sport. You can tell if a person if giving it their all, or if their heart isn't completely in it, so I try and

give 110% every class I attend because I absolutely love karate. Grading isn't a competition, and it's not all about who can reach black belt the quickest - it's all about humility and being the best version of you possible, and progressing at an appropriate speed. I do collect Sammo Hung's movies on DVD, VCD and Blu-Ray, having started back in 2019 after a spontaneous visit to a second hand store in Glasgow with a friend netted me a copy of Project A on DVD. Since then, my collection has spiraled, and I constantly keep an eye out in charity shops and on eBay for new additions. There is one lone VHS in my collection, and that's a copy of Heart of Dragon that I found on eBay for about £2 or so (because the case was damaged). Since Heart of Dragon is my favorite Sammo film, and the one that started my journey in the first place, I happen to have 5 copies of it across varying formats - VHS, DVD, VCD and two different Blu-Rays (one from Hong Kong, the other is the 88 Films release from a couple of years back). Unless I buy a VHS player in the future, which is highly unlikely given that (quite unfortunately) the VHS is now obsolete, I most likely will not be adding any more VHS tapes to my collection. At current, I only have one laserdisc in my collection, despite the fact that I do not own a laserdisc player and do not plan on buying one in the near future (a region free Blu-Ray player would be a better investment, as far as I am concerned).

At the time of writing this piece, I have not long passed my 2nd kyu grading exam. I have a lucky shirt with Sammo on it that I wear under my gi to my exams, which I only ever wear for exams. Hopefully Sammo Hung will continue to be my source of inspiration and admiration until I sit my 1st Dan black belt, and for as long as I continue training in Shotokan karate.

*Note in the photos of me the purple/white belt was my 4th kyu belt and the brown belt is my current (2nd kyu) belt.

Cynthia ROTHROCK
The Blonde Fury
Interviewed by Rick Baker
羅芙洛

About Cynthia

Cynthia was World Champion in forms and weapons five times between 1981 and 1985. These categories are not combat-oriented, being displays of fluidity of movement rather than fighting, and are not segregated into male and female categories but fully open to both sexes.

She took first place in forms 32 times and first place in weapons 12 times in her first 38 tournaments, including competing in "Men's Forms" three out of four times as there was no Women's Division. She was "Grand Master" of five tournaments and came in first place in 4 out of 5 fighting events. She holds seven black belts and sashes in multiple Far Eastern martial disciplines, including Tang Soo Do, Taekwondo (Korean), Eagle Claw (Chinese), Wushu, Northern Shaolin, Ng Ying Kungfu (Chinese: □□□□), and Pai Lum White Dragon Kung Fu. She received her 6th degree black belt in Tang Soo Do Moo Duk Kwan in 2006. She was tested by Grand Master Robert Kovaleski, 9th Dan and chair of the I.T.M.A., and was later promoted by him to 7th degree black belt in 2011 and 8th degree black belt in 2015.[8] She is a martial arts instructor and her favourite weapons are the hook swords.

Cynthia is no stranger to the pages of "Eastern Heroes" and she was kind enough to catch up with me during her busy schedule to talk about her career and pay respect to the portly kicker that is Sammo Hung

RB: Did movies inspire you to start martial arts?

CR: No. I started doing martial arts and I didn't even know what it was. I didn't watch any martial arts movies. My friend at the time had parents who practised martial arts. I watched them and thought, wow, what is that? I want to do that! I've always been an 'out of the box' person and this was right up my street. It wasn't until a couple of years later that I was introduced to kung fu movies and started studying under Shum Leung in Chinatown in New York.

RB: There was a boom in popularity when Enter the Dragon came out. Schools had to hire bigger halls just to cope with the increase in interest!

CR: Yeah. I remember I wanted to learn kung fu. I was studying karate and I saw a book by Donnie Yen's mother, Bow-sim Mark. She was one of the first women I'd seen do kung fu. Before I studied under Shum Leung, I went to Chinatown and found a White Crane school. They didn't want to accept me at first because they didn't want any Caucasian people there. Nevertheless, they let me in. We had to go and study in the basement!

RB: Back in the day, it was very rare to be accepted.

CR: It wasn't a money-maker. All the instructors had other jobs. It was a hobby. You had to have toughness credentials to stick it out. One teacher told me that if they didn't like someone, they kicked the crap out of them so they'd leave! I remember when I was testing for my black belt, and some Koreans came to test us. They said, 'Your students don't know how to fight.' So, for three weeks they fought us every single day. I'd go home, limping, and covered in bruises.

RB: You wouldn't get away with that today with health and safety!

CR: I know! I said to my instructor, 'Are you trying to get rid of me?' I'll tell you what, though. From that day on, I was never afraid to fight. I remember one of my instructors had an electric cattle prod that he used to use if you weren't low down enough in horse stance.

RB: Really?! That sounds like Drunken Master!

CR: Oh yeah. It was tough! I think that's why I'm so tough now!

RB: Did you start training in other schools as you got older?

CR: Yeah. I started off in Tang Soo Do. A friend was studying Pai Lum kung fu, and I liked the movements and low stances. It seemed like it fitted me a little bit better, so I started studying both. We are talking about a time when people would come into your school and challenge you.

RB: Really?

CR: Yes! We had that many times. I had to choose one style or the other, so I chose the kung fu. Then, while competing, I saw Sham Leung, and I was desperate to learn the double-headed spear form. Weapons are something that, even today, are my favourite. So then I was doing Eagle Claw, and I saw Wushu, and I just had to do that, too. I moved from the East Coast to the West Coast to study that. In 1982 I trained in Wushu in China for eight weeks. I was in heaven!

RB: I know a few people have told me that you get the most authentic training experience in China. I guess that foundation must be locked into you?

CR: Oh yeah, definitely.
RB: It's the difference between people who are serious and people who lose interest. If it's locked into you and you have the focus, it's lifelong. I brought Hwang Jang Lee over to the UK, and he still has it all. He's in his seventies! He's a lovely guy.

CR: He is. I did No Retreat No Surrender with him. We shot that film for about five months and became good friends. I didn't see him for ages after that, but I started to go back to my Tang Soo Do roots, and travelled to Korea. We had to perform for all the masters. I always thought Hwang Jang Lee had a taekwondo background, but I was looking at all the masters grading us, and I was like, 'Is that Hwang Jang Lee?' He was looking at me, and I was like 'Oh my God!' I didn't even know he was a master in Tang Soo Do! I couldn't believe it.

RB: When he came over, he didn't think anyone would know who he was! He has so many fans, though, and they turned up because they loved the old films.

CR: Oh yeah, he's the Silver Fox, right?

RB: Exactly! He had a translator, but I remember asking him if he thought Invincible Armour was his best film, and he said, 'Rick, I've never even watched these!' After we did that event, though, he suddenly realised he was liked, and that he could have a career travelling around, meeting fans.

CR: I did an event with him in Trinidad, and they all loved The Silver Fox!

RB: So, let's get onto Sammo Hung. Did you only ever do one film with him?

CR: I did Shanghai Express with him, and he had a small part in Yes, Madam.

RB: That's right! How did you get the part in Shanghai Express?

CR: When I went to Hong Kong I thought I would do Yes, Madam, and that would be it. I thought I'd maybe be on the poster and be able to show my kids that their mom had been in a movie.

RB: Why were you even in Hong Kong? How did you get into the industry?

CR: Well, I owe it all to Yuen Kwai. I was on the West Coast demonstration team, and he was working with Ng See-yuen at Seasonal Films. Ng See-yuen wanted Corey to go to the United States to find a guy that was going to be the next Bruce Lee. They called up Ernie Reyes on the West Coast demonstration team. I was on the team, and Ernie said, 'Should I bring the girls, or just the guys?' Paul Maslak, the editor of Inside

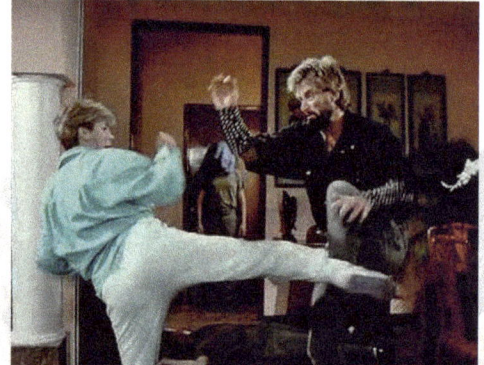

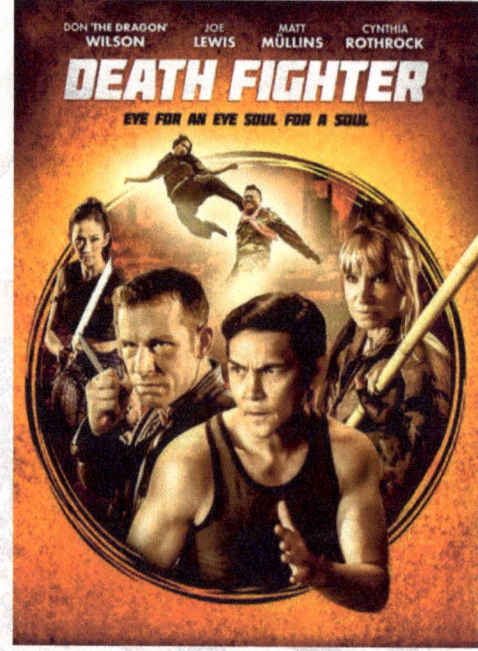

Kung Fu, suggested taking the girls too. We went down to Beverly Hills and I had to do some self-defence and some weapons work. Corey Yuen said, 'I want to go with the girl!' That's how it started.

RB: Fantastic.

CR: I did Yes, Madam, came back, and straight away got calls from studios that wanted to sign me up for a three-picture deal, such as Golden Harvest.

RB: Had you aspired to be a movie star before that opportunity?

CR: No. I hadn't even thought of it! I was teaching martial arts, so I thought that was my path. I was really focusing on my competition at that time, because I had a goal that I wanted to be undefeated for five years, then retire as number one. The same year that I did Yes, Madam, I was into the fifth year of that. I had competed in over a hundred tournaments and was undefeated. Ranking was based on a points system, so I kept telling Yuen Kwai that I had to go back to compete. I didn't want to lose sight of my goal. I'd trained so hard!

RB: That's so admirable because some people would have just ditched it for the movie career.

CR: When I finished Yes, Madam, I retired from competition undefeated. I knew I could focus on the movies then. It was a smooth transition.

RB: How did you get onto Shanghai Express?

CR: Sammo said he wanted to use me in his next movie.

RB: Were you aware of how big a deal he was in Hong Kong cinema?

CR: Yeah! I knew when I agreed to do Shanghai Express that I'd have to fight Sammo. All the stunt people were telling me how hard he was to fight. They were like, 'I feel sorry for you.'

RB: He hits hard!

CR: Yes, he was hard to fight, but not as hard as I thought. I think because everyone was amping me up, saying he was so big and so strong, you know? The hardest person I've ever fought was in The Blonde Fury. The Thai Fighter.

RB: Was that Billy Chow?

CR: That's right, Billy Chow. That was tough. He was so hard that they made metal arm guards for me. I was wearing them while we fought, and they were hurting him! So they made metal arm guards for him, too. We were fighting metal on metal. In Hong Kong they don't film with any sound, and it's a good thing, because all you could hear was clanging!

RB: How did you find Sammo when you met him?

CR: I was nervous. He didn't speak English, and I didn't speak Chinese. I just knew that Chinese stuntmen were afraid to fight him. Then, I'm fighting him in this scene where I have a dress on, and I'm thinking, 'Oh my gosh, I can't put pads on my legs!' He kicked my shins so many times and it was brutal. It's pretty realistic fighting in Hong Kong.

RB: How did he communicate the choreography?

CR: We rehearsed, but it was on the day. It wasn't a case of, 'Here's a couple of days to practise this.' We always did it right on set, right before we were going to shoot.

RB: That's the Hong Kong way.

CR: Yeah! And you know what? I could do it. At that time I could do a hundred forms. My memory was really good. On those films we might have twenty-five moves all in one take, all really fast, but I could remember them. So I think that's one of the reasons I kept getting offers to do more films. Not only was it unusual for a Caucasian girl to be fighting in Hong Kong, I could also do what they asked, and I was tough. I didn't complain or cry.

RB: Do you think Sammo was impressed?

CR: I think so. I remember that Richard Norton and I were meant to be from the Confederate army, and they told us that we had to wear three layers of clothes because it was winter. Never did I think, 'You're not seeing the three layers! You're only seeing the outer set!' So it was boiling and we were sweating, and I looked bigger than I was. I didn't have the experience to question it.

RB: Was it a good experience?

CR: Absolutely. I think Sammo and Yuen Kwai are geniuses at martial arts choreography. I was just so impressed working with them. I was working with the best of the best, The Steven Spielberg of martial arts films.

RB: How long was the shoot?

CR: About two and a half months. That was quick, because Yes, Madam was seven and a half months. Sammo shot Shanghai Express round the clock. Sometimes we'd film for 24 hours. We'd go home, shower, and come right back. I remember falling asleep on the set because we were up almost two days. Sammo had a deadline to get it finished for Chinese New Year. I recall the make-up artist waking me up, saying, 'Cynthia, you'll have bags under your eyes!'

RB: That film became a cult classic. It was the first film I ever screened. The audience went crazy! Did you keep in touch with Sammo?

CR: I did for a while. I'd love to do something with Sammo again. And Yuen Biao and Yuen Kwai!

RB: Well! There all still active so opportunity could knock.

As always I would like to thank you for taking out the time to chat and look forward to doing a follow up on your career in a future issue and the possibility of bringing you over to the UK in the near future.

CR: Look forward to it

PAINTED FACES

The movie posters of Sammo Hung, 1977-1984
By Alan Donkin

"Oh great. Another piece on posters by that know-nothing imbecile."
I know, I know. It's kinda my thing. I'm going to take a look at the theatrical posters of Sammo's films, and decide on a favourite. I'll apologise in advance to anyone who hasn't flicked immediately to the next article. Actually, it's a three-fold apology.
1) It's not a comprehensive look at all of his posters over that period. There's just too many.
2) It's not a look at posters from other territories. Same reason as number 1. Homers only, I'm afraid.
3) I have to be upfront. I'm not a massive fan of the cartoon art stuff. I'm trying to appreciate it more. This piece will be part of that education process. So, you're all (the five of you who've struggled to this point) essentially reading an art-appreciation seminar delivered for me, by me. Lucky you. Not a great start, really, but if you'll allow me a moment to elaborate? I've decided to look at only sixteen of Sammo's film posters between the years of 1977 and 1984. Why those years? The reason is partly selfish. It's part of the classic era of kung fu movies, which is my favourite era. So why not include his early 70s output? Well, many of his roles prior to 1977 weren't what I'd consider to be 'lead' roles. He wasn't the star in a consecutive run of films.
In addition to those considerations, I had to stop at 1984 due to the format of this article. I thought it would be quite fun to create a knockout (or should that be Knockabout?) tournament. Pitting poster against poster. Assessing their artistic merits and deciding on a victor to progress to the next round, until eventually we are left with a final, and then an overall winner. A round of sixteen to start with would ensure a simple whittling down via head-to-head duels. By 1984, I'd already made sixteen picks. There's also the fact that if I'd included Eastern Condors in the selection, the whole thing would be rigged by Ricky.
I've used an online randomiser to make it a fair tournament. About three seconds into the development of this idea I realised it was a pretty stupid one, because you could match two absolutely stunning posters in the first round, thus eliminating an absolute corker early doors. At the same time, two dog turds could duke it out, guaranteeing the presence of excrement in an advanced stage of the tournament.
Who cares? It's only a bit of a laugh. It's not an ordered top 16. Anyway, regardless of the format, we'd disagree. That's part of the beauty of looking at these film posters. Opinions differ, and it would be a very dull world if we all agreed on everything. Just don't expect a cartoony one to win.
Let's move onto Round One, Battle One.
FIGHT!

The Magnificent Butcher (1979) vs The Victim (1980)

For crying out loud. That fear I had about eliminating a belter in the first round? It's going to happen. First, though, I have to make what could be an unpopular decision. The Magnificent Butcher has three variants to my knowledge. One features, as its centrepiece, the iconic scene between Kwan Tak-Hing and Lee Hoi-Sang, as they duel using paintbrushes. For me, this scene is the best in the entire movie. It's a glorious balance of passive-aggressive posturing and respect for the martial code. It's a duel with very little visceral aggression – just superiority using core skills. The creativity on show is astonishing, with both combatants benefitting from the incredibly choreography of Yuen Wo-Ping and Sammo. The poster shows the Kwan and Lee locked together, like two Angels of the North back-to-back, vying for supremacy.
The second variant relegates that scene to the foot of the poster, huddled with all the other bits and bobs that made up the bottom of the first variant. In its place is a huge image of a smirking Sammo as Butcher Wing, whose arms are taken by two pigs. It's the oddest Punch and Judy show you'll ever see. I have to admit, it's not my favourite image. I know it has its fans, but to me it just looks plain weird. There's nothing wrong with the Sammo rendition – it captures him really well – it's just not overly-appealing to see a pig act as his battle gloves and gauntlets.
The third variant balances the first two images – with each being given prime

real-estate space in the central portion of the poster. This is the best version in my eyes. It satisfies fans of both images, and the main font style in the top left is the most in-keeping with the hurried, sketchy writing

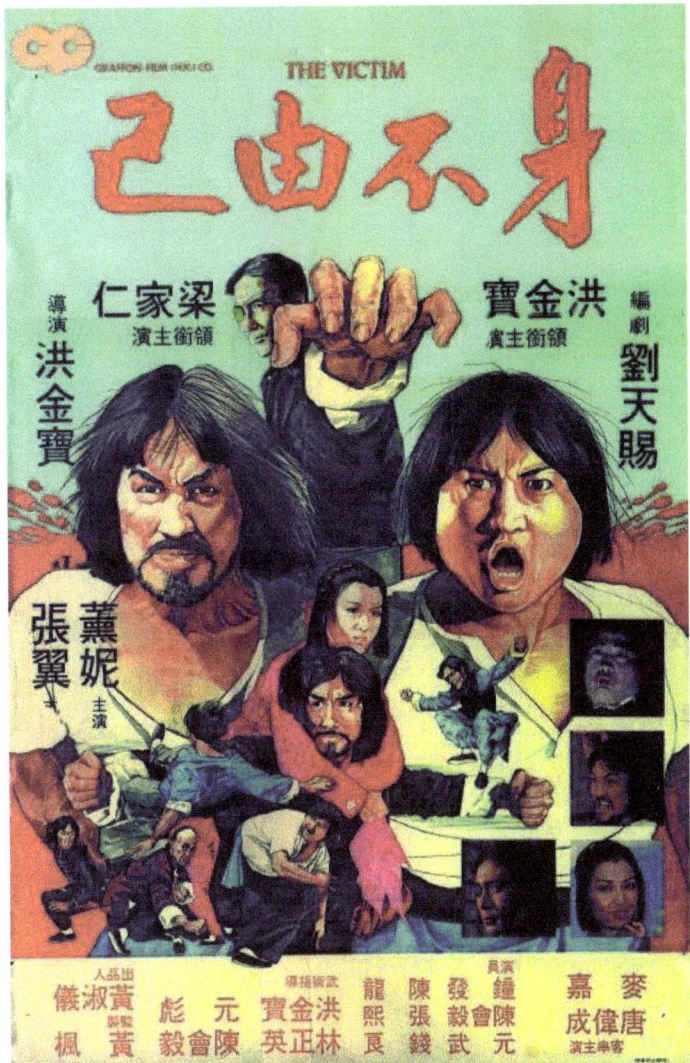

of that iconic calligraphy scene, albeit in a different colour. For the purposes of this battle, this third variant is the one I'll use. The poster has an absolutely superb art-style, emphasising heavy, thick outlining in places. Years later, that style would be a fad in computer game art design, under the banner of 'cel-shading'. The Magnificent Butcher design is so, so much more. There's both a vague sketchiness to the people AND a level of detail which makes them expressive and instantly recognisable. The drawings have a suggestion of cartoonishness to them, but they could also be rotoscoped animations using photos, like the work in A Scanner Darkly (2006). The colour palette is beautiful, mixing both soft and deep watercolours to add real movement and depth to the snapshots. The entire image is fantastically well-balanced, creating a montage of memorable scenes from the film. The way the colours are 'held' by the variable-thickness outlining is a feast for the eyes.

The Magnificent Butcher is going to take some beating. Step forward The Victim, which is a wholly-different proposition. I mean, come on. It's class, isn't it? What's not to like? We've got striking drawings of Sammo and Leung Kar-Yan looking well 'ard. You can see the fury in their faces. Even their necks seem taut with aggression. There's drawings AND photos of the cast at the foot of the poster. An explosion of blood takes up half the background. Stunning! Although ... look more closely. There's certain things about this poster that, on greater inspection, look slightly 'off'. Sammo and Beardy's faces don't seem quite in tune with their bodies, like their faces have been grafted onto the torsos of someone else. The general font styles are pretty dull. And Chang Yi's arm and hand extending towards the protagonists suffers from perspective issues. It's a good-enough drawing, but it seems to me to be slightly too low down, or too far away from his body. I can't decide. It reminds me of the Ozzy Osbourne character in Bo' Selecta with the massive arms. I know the whole design is meant to be based around anger and skulduggery, but it's very in-your-face.

VERDICT: Subtlety and balance triumph over raw anger, and The Magnificent

Page 39   Eastern Heroes Sammo Hung Special

Butcher progresses to the quarter finals. The Victim is a great poster, with fantastic renditions of the two heroes showcasing real emotion, but The Magnificent Butcher oozes class in so many ways.

Round One, Battle Two.

Odd Couple (1979) vs Winners and Sinners (1983)

This one is more straightforward. Odd Couple is a stunning poster. I remember the first time I saw it on eBay. I bid far higher than I ought to have, but was blown away by someone who clearly wanted it more. I mentioned to Ray Farrell (who has kindly allowed me to use some of his poster photos in this article) that I'd missed out on it, and how gutted I was. He said that he'd seen it, missed out on it, and was equally gutted. Imagine my surprise/horror when he messaged me a while later to say that his wife had won the auction and bought it as a gift for him! See – that's the level of love this poster encourages. I jest – Ray is a fantastic bloke and I'm very glad that this poster found its way into his collection.

Take a look at it. Have you ever seen a similar design? In my experience, it's singularly striking. The artwork isn't what I'd call realistic, but it leans into that camp more than the goofball art of other Sammo posters. The poster is divided into two sections by the spear and sabre - weapons which feature prominently in the film. A flash of red acts as a counterpoint to the lime green and yellow/sepia colours that dominate the page. The image is arranged like a duel, only breaking rank at the very bottom, as Dean Shek presents his weasel routine to punters. It's a highly-effective arrangement that models the concept of the film – two masters who can't be separated training their students to settle their score. I really like how the two faces are the central focus of the poster, yet they don't overwhelm everything else. Your eyes are still drawn elsewhere. In contrast, Winners and Sinners is slightly dull. It's a pleasant design, but nothing that really grabs the eyeballs and demands attention. There's not a great deal going on. Some might argue that frugality is a strength, but I'd say that a film as good as

this deserves better. The big-head montage doesn't really entice or engage, and the action snapshots are tiny, showing what appear to be 1980s Micro Machines. It sounds like I have a right downer on this poster. I don't, I just find it utterly forgettable.

VERDICT: Winner: Odd Couple. Loser: Winners.
Sorry, it's a no-brainer for this judge.

Round One, Battle Three.

Wheels on Meals (1984) vs The Incredible Kung Fu Master (1984)

Dilemma: which variant do I pick? The Three Musketeers one? Or the one with Sammo in a straitjacket? I twisted and turned for about twenty minutes over this. I prefer the colours of the straitjacket one, but the arrangement of the fencing design. Sammo wears a ridiculous John McCririck hat in both designs (Google him, non-British readers!), but looks rather muted and pathetic in the second variant. His posture and expression is meaner on the first variant, but Jackie is wearing a ridiculous black vest that mutes the power of the trio. Eventually, I settled on the second variant, because the blue provides such a striking background. Artistically, it's highly-competent. Although drawings, the faces err more on the side of realism than caricature. The first variant is perhaps too symmetrical, whereas the second nods towards the concept but isn't a slave to it. There's plenty going on, but the design isn't swamped. The sectioning-off of the title at the bottom really works for me – if imposed over the pictures, it would seem too cluttered. The clouds in the background add a softness to the brightness of the blue, and the introduction of yellow via the vehicle complements the title font colour nicely. I've re-written this section on The Incredible Kung Fu Master three times. It started out very critical, but the more I looked at it, the more I appreciated it. At first, my views were coloured by the fact that the whole concept screams 'UNFUNNY COMEDY' of the kind with which I've firmly lost my tolerance. After a while, I managed to put that aside. The drawing style is rather sweet, and the street in the background very nicely drawn. The expressions of the characters are skilfully sketched and shaded. The artist has done a fine job. It's just that, overall, it lacks something. I can't pinpoint what. Perhaps it's the outer

section of the poster? It's a tad dull and unremarkable.

VERDICT: This was a far closer bout than I originally envisaged. I've grown rather fond of Kung Fu Master since I've taken the time to really study it. It's not 'too cartoony' for me, and it has a warmth that I appreciate. Wheels on Meals takes it, though, by the width of a thin cracker.

Round One, Battle Four.

Dirty Tiger, Crazy Frog (1978) vs The Iron Fisted Monk (1977)
Awesome. Another cartoony one. I'm finding the endless parade of this style somewhat wearying. I'll try and be fair, though. It's a decent design, I can't deny it. The stars are very nicely-drawn, with amusing expressions and postures. The tiger and frog images are super, and the way they reflect their human counterpoints below is very effective. Everything is symmetrically-arranged and competent. But that's all I can say about it, really. I'm sorry. It's a good poster, but I can't get excited about it.
Iron Fisted Monk is a great film, and one of those where I feel that the poster should be so much better. It's a strong design, but missing something. I'll lay down the good stuff first. The colour choices are excellent, offering a stark, eye-catching simplicity. The use of photos is nicely-handled, too. The large images are blended into the blue background, with their full colour twins taking up the lower portion of the page. There's just something unremarkable about the whole thing. The weird lines through the blue-toned photo are just grating. I believe it's called the moire effect? It's like when you take a photo of a computer screen. I can only assume it's a conscious design decision, but as Graham Taylor said, do I not like that. I can't help but wonder how good this poster could have been if produced by Golden Harvest in the early 70s.

VERDICT: Iron Fisted Monk shades this duel, almost by default. I'm too bored with the caricatures. In fairness, it's a genuinely nice design, just a bit of a missed opportunity.

Round One, Battle Five.
Enter the Fat Dragon (1978) vs Close Encounter of the Spooky Kind (1980)

What did I expect? 'Enter the Fat Dragon.'

Sigh. It's not a bad design, really. The hairy, fat stomach and trotters are hilarious, and the little fights taking place underneath are great. The photo of Bruce is a fab little nod to the great man, and there's an air of self-aware fun about the whole thing. I really don't like Sammo's nose, though.
Spooky Kind is a totally different kettle of fish. Alright, it's another montage of cartoons, but before the hypocritical card gets thrown at me, just take a look at the sheer ostentatiousness of the design. Bright, bold colours are thrown in your face, with little snippets of action kicking off all over. It's so busy, but not in an overwhelming way.

Every time I look, I see something different. The black background is the clincher. It wouldn't work with a white background – the black frames everything beautifully.

VERDICT: Spooky, easily. It's a unique effort and really makes you sit up and take notice. That's the job of a poster, right? Round One, Battle Six.

Filthy Guy (1978) vs Project A (1983)

Filthy Guy is one of those rare posters where I'd have to think twice about accepting a copy for free. Look at it. It's plug ugly. A

desperately unremarkable selection of photographs over a terrible combination of background colours. Sammo looks like he's curling out a particularly satisfying whippy in the primary shot, which sums it up. The only saving grace is Carter Wong's boot-to-the-face photo. The perspective of the photo is interesting, and it actually makes the film look like more than an assemblage of buffoonery.

Project A has a couple of variants. The first shows Jackie on his bike and Sammo with a tab hanging from his mouth. It's ok. I'm not keen on the background stuff, to be honest. A far better variant is the more well-known one, which shows our three leads given equal billing in a striking line-up in the bottom half of the poster. Even though they're bobbleheads, they're really-well drawn. The colouration of the faces is superb, and their stances charismatic. The thing that makes the poster stand out is the background. It's a hand-drawn snapshot of an amazing action sequence, stunningly rendered. We aren't talking about a few blokes duking it out in a void. The full environment is included, affording the image a real sense of context. The care and attention on show is laudable – the painting, statue and windows are all skilfully rendered by an artist who has gone to great lengths to produce something that stands out from the crowd.

VERDICT: Filthy Guy wins. Actually, even joking about it makes me feel queasy. Project A wipes the floor with the opposition. One poster throws together a lazy montage of photos, whereas the other demonstrates how things should be done.

Round One, Battle Seven.

Knockabout (1979) vs Warriors Two (1978)

Curse that damn random fixture generator! It's pitted 'like' against 'like' in the cruellest way possible. I've already raved about the art style used here while taking about the Magnificent Butcher efforts. It's just glorious, and a real halcyon patch for Golden Harvest posters. Almost everything about the Knockabout poster is superb. The sketched fights are energetic and contain that element of perspective that provided the Filthy Guy poster with a rare moment of quality. The character moments are drawn thoughtfully, their watercolours sensitive, yet powerful. The only issue I have is the (comparatively) dull upper half of the poster. It's too sparse and bland, especially the white expanses in the top left.

Warriors Two suffers no such malaise. It's stupidly well-balanced, with nothing I'd consider to be 'dead space'. Again, the artwork is first-rate. The stacked images burst from the poster with raw energy, and there's even enough space for a thoughtful grey and white watercolour scene in the background. The gold font used is gorgeous, and the way thin black lines are used to separate the text is genius. The whole poster has a modern, clinical look to it, but it's far from soulless. This should feature in everyone's collection.

VERDICT: Knockabout is brilliant, but Warriors Two is even better. Eye-wateringly majestic.

Round One, Battle Eight.
The Prodigal Son (1981) vs The Dead and the Deadly (1982)
For me, The Prodigal Son exemplifies those films where you follow this experience: You hear about the movie. You hunt it out. You watch it. You love it. It's a classic. You look at the poster art. You're massively underwhelmed. See also: Eight Diagram Pole Fighter. Prodigal Son even has two stabs at getting it right, and both fall short. The first is the sketched effort. It's alright, but is there anything to get excited about? Not really. Compared to the wonders of Battle Seven, it's all a bit subdued and tepid. Nothing really happens in the poster. Even the single piece of martial arts action on show has all the excitement and energy of a Downing Street press conference. I can appreciate the decent quality of the likenesses, but the whole thing is presented like a comic strip that no-one can be bothered to read, and the artist knows it. The second variant sounds more interesting if I were to describe it, but in reality, it's not all that great. The photo selections are decent, especially the flame-filled long shot at the top, but generally the design is a little dull. I don't know if it's the face paints. They just don't set my world alight. The general darkness of the gaps makes it a more effective poster than the other variant, but I can't say that it's a poster that I look at and feel wowed by.
The Dead and the Deadly, on the other hand, is a poster to which I feel more drawn. It's unfussy and striking, with a huge image of Sammo commanding the centre of the design. He is surrounded by things that intrigue and snare interest. I particularly like the background colour, and the way it blends sky blue into black. The only things that grate are the over-dominance of blue, which creates a clothing/backdrop clash, and the almost-hidden yellow font English title in the bottom corner. I mean, just don't bother if that's the best you can do.

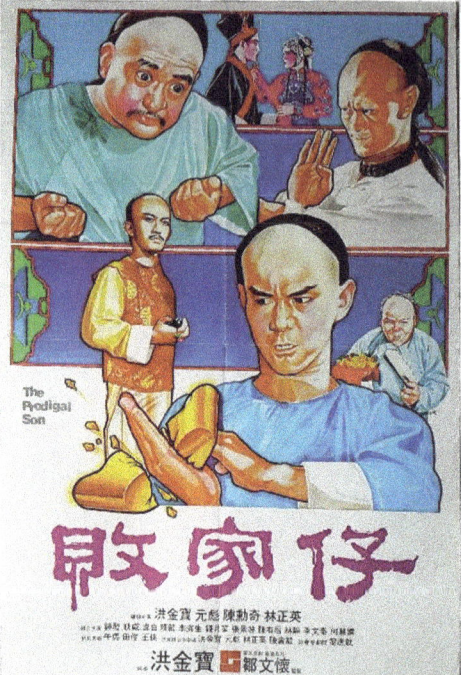

VERDICT: It doesn't really matter which version of The Prodigal Son I select. Both lose out to The Dead and the Deadly. It could benefit from more subtlety and darkness in places, but it's generally the superior design.

Quarter Final, Battle One.

The Iron Fisted Monk (1977) vs The Magnificent Butcher (1979)
This isn't even a competition. The only thing Iron Fisted Monk has over its opponent is that gorgeous blue background. The skill and creativity in the Magnificent Butcher design places it head and shoulders above its foe. One looks lazy, the other is a feast of quality.

VERDICT:
The Magnificent Butcher rams a calligraphy pen up the nose of The Iron Fisted Monk.

Quarter Final, Battle Two
Project A (1983) vs The Dead and the Deadly (1982)
When I prepped this article by hand, I had

Deadly down as the winner. But studying these posters in greater detail during the writing process has changed my mind. Project A doesn't stray into the dreaded territory of comedy caricature bantz – it's a beautiful, balanced design that, on closer inspection, reveals layers of quality. The action sequence in the background clinches it.

VERDICT: Like a 1980s overweight comedy circuit veteran, Deadly is just too blue. Project A is a finely-tuned study of charisma and action.

Quarter Final, Battle Three.

Odd Couple (1979) vs Warriors Two (1978)

I legitimately could have cried when the computer spat out this matchup. Two absolute stunners. How do you choose? I had to revert back to basics. Which poster would I rather have? Odd Couple, by a shade (which, of course, I don't have). The design is so unique, and really smacks your eyes full-whack like the pussies they are.

VERDICT: Warriors Two is amazing, but there are other similar designs, so Odd Couple wins on a points decision.
Quarter Final, Battle Four.
Wheels on Meals (1984) vs Close Encounter of the Spooky Kind (1980)
Side-by-side, it's a tough call. It's like tasting chalk and cheese. But who the hell eats chalk? Both posters have their merits and their drawbacks. Wheels on Meals is so bright and cartoony, it could be a Nintendo game. Spooky is so busy that it's like an exploding kaleidoscope.

VERDICT: Spooky, just. It's more interesting on the eye. If the Wheels on Meals poster were a mate, it would be that sunny side up gobby one, that calls itself 'bubbly' and has a 'Live Laugh Love' plaque in the kitchen. It would annoy you after a bit. Spooky is the joyful friend who has a fascinating dark edge. It probably listens to Joy Division records while dressed as Timmy Mallett.

Semi Final, Battle One.

Close Encounter of the Spooky Kind (1980) vs The Magnificent Butcher (1979)

These are like yin and yang. I really do love the Spooky poster, but there's a time when the attention-seekers get too overpowering, and you just want them to bugger off so you can enjoy something a bit more sedate and measured.

VERDICT: Sammo's Magnificent Butcher unleashes a haymaker in the eighth round, revelling coolly in the triumph of another big scalp, while Spooky slinks off to the dressing room to lick its wounds. It was a brave effort, but the artistic brilliance of Butcher is just too powerful to defend against.

Semi Final, Battle Two.

Odd Couple (1979) vs Project A (1983)

The kinetic brilliance of the Odd Couple poster, alongside its colour palette, give it the edge over most posters, and this bout is no different. It's a shame because I've really grown to love the Project A poster, from a position of absolute indifference.

VERDICT: Project A's brave journey is over, but the plucky underdog has won a new fan. It's the flagbearer to which all bobblehead designs should aspire. Odd Couple is still the poster that I'd prefer, though.

THE FINAL!

Odd Couple (1979) vs The Magnificent Butcher (1979)

The hardest decision of my life. That's a lie, but c'mon. This is so difficult. I look at both posters carefully, and then I make a decision. Then I look again, and make the opposite decision. Repeat ad infinitum, unless I make a call.

VERDICT: The watercolours and the variable black outlines of The Magnificent Butcher are just too good to ignore. Everything about the design oozes class. Winner: The Magnificent Butcher (1979) When I came up with this idea for an article, I pictured this in my top four. I've had a great time looking at other posters in greater depth, but I keep coming back to this one. It's even better than I remembered. A worthy champion!

Interview with Robert "Bobby" Samuels

By Simon Pritchard

Robert Samuels, also known as Bobby, is an actor and a martial artist from the heyday of 1990's Hong Kong cinema to modern action thrillers. Bobby has worked on films such as "John Wick 3: Chapter 3 – Parabellum". When working on "The Matrix" (1999), Laurence Fishburne based Morpheous's character and spirituality on Bobby. Bobby has most recently stared in the lead role in 2022's "Jugando Con Fuego".

From a child Bobby trained in Hung Gar kung fu under Chi-Ling Chiu and then wanted to progress into acting. Whilst Hollywood was employing action stars; Bobby went to auditions and released and he wanted to differentiate himself from the other actors. Growing up Bobby was inspired by such Legends as Jim Kelly, Lo Lieh and Grandmaster Ron Van Clief; Bobby knew that Grandmaster Ron Van Clief had been successful in China. Being fluent in Chinese, his martial art abilities and acting skills; Bobby packed his bags and went to Hong Kong.

In 1987 Bobby landed his first role in "The Good, The Bad, The Beauty" starring Frankie Chan, Bobby starred in "Fatal Bet" in 1989 and was an assistant stunt coordinator on "She Shoots Straight" in 1990. That's where the story begins….

SP: How were you introduced to Sammo? Do you remember your first meeting?

RS: Yes so, the first time I met Sammo was a very unusual situation. At the time Chi Ling Chu was representing me in Hong Kong.

We decided to have lunch in Tsim Sha Choi. I went to the bathroom and I'm washing my hands at the sink and in walks a Shaw Brothers veteran Cheng Hong Yip. I immediately recognized him and spoke to him in Cantonese. He was shocked. He asked jokingly "What was a black American doing in Hong Kong?" I told him I wanted to do movies he was shocked at my answer and I said that I was not leaving Hong Kong until I do.

He then asked me what was I doing later that evening, I said I was free. He then said to meet him at the Niko Hotel at 7pm. I got there early and waited for like 15 minutes, then in walks Chen Kuan Tai and Cheng Hong Yip. We order coffee I was in shock. I was a big fan of Chen Kuan Tai and Cheng Hong Yip. We ordered coffee then Cheng Hong Yip said we need to wait for one more person to come. About five minutes later I see Sammo Hung walking to our table. I almost had a panic attack!

He comes and sits with us and I introduced myself. Paul Cheng explained to him what I wanted to do. I had some photos with me of myself in action. I showed Sammo and he took the photos and started going through them. He asked me if I could fight, I said "yes". He said can you fight four or five guys at the same time. I said "yeah" that was all he said. He stayed for around 20 minutes then he said he had to go. I was crushed I felt as though I made a bad impression on him.

SP: Your first film with Sammo was "Gambling Ghost" (1991) also starring Yuen Biao. What role did you have and how did Sammo notice you?

RS: After first meeting him at the Niko Hotel Paul said "let's go get some dinner there was someone else he wanted me to meet" We all went to a seafood restaurant in Kowloon City. As Chen Kuan Tai, Paul and I were eating, in walks Lily Li another Shaw Brothers veteran. She sat down and Paul introduced me. I felt like I was living in a dream that night. As we were eating Paul's phone rang. He was talking to someone but I had no idea. When he hung up he looked at me and said "I have some news for you", I said "what was it?" He said that was Sammo, he had decided to change the ending on a film he was staring in called "Gambling Ghost". I almost pasted out! I was so deeply grateful for Paul and all he did for a man he really didn't even know, my life changed that night.

SP: After "Gambling Ghost", you moved in with Sammo for approximately four years. How did this come about?

RS: After I did "Gambling Ghost" I went back to the States .I went back to my job at USAirways for another six months. I then got a call from Sammo saying he was coming to New York and he wanted me to meet him at the airport. I was so excited that he reached out to me.

He was renting a house in Old Westbury, New York, a house that had horses and a lot of land. I met him and we went to the house and set up everything. This was also my first time meeting Yuen Biao. He flew in several days later to meet with Sammo at the house. I stayed with him the entire time he was there and then he went back to Hong Kong.

Before he left he said if I ever needed him he would be there for me. His words meant so much to me. I go back home and work at the airport for another six months. I'm at work one day and they called me into the office and said they were going to do layoffs and I was going to be let go. I was so depressed. I knew that was God's way of saying now is the time. I called Sammo and told him I was going to lose my job at the airline. He said "Don't worry catch the first

plane out to Hong Kong". He would help me.

I knew this was my last chance to save my dreams. I bought a one way ticket to Hong Kong and I didn't want to come back without achieving my goals. When I arrived in Hong Kong, Sammo took me to the immigration department and said I would be his English teacher on the books. He then told them I would be living with him at his house. He then put me on a contract at Bojon Films, his company. That's when my life really changed forever.

SP: Did you train regularly with Sammo? What styles did you learn with and from him?

RS: So yes, I trained with him & Leung Chia Yan quite often. Sammo had his own Action Team and I trained with them all the time. One notable member, who is my brother, was Colin Chou Ngai Sing from the "The Matrix" (1999). He and I spent the most time together because we were the same age and had the same birthday, August 11th. Colin Chou was my main teacher on the Stunt team. We were like blood brothers and both of us were the only two students Sammo had at that time.

SP: What was it like day-to-day? You must have some awesome experiences and seen some amazing films being made. What do you remember about this?

RS: Every day I had to report to Bojon Films. I had to get there before Sammo came to make sure he had everything he needed to start the day. So many celebrities of Hong Kong cinema was at the office every day. Basically we were always developing ideas for future projects. At this time I was not doing films, I basically was his bodyguard. Wherever he went, I went. The local media thought he was in some kind of trouble with the Triads and thought I was hired to protect him! LOL! It was not the case. Sammo had done so much for me allowing me to live with his family. I didn't realize how much people paid attention to me until I would go somewhere on my own. The People of Hong Kong recognized me everywhere. The paparazzi were always filming Sammo and I was with him, so I was treated very well because everyone knew I was Sammo Hung's guy.

SP: Where there ever any difficult situations when protecting Sammo?

RS: Not really Sammo is "Daai Gaw" (Big

Brother). NO ONE ever tried anything because of the level of respect the country had for Sammo & Jackie Chan. He was a national treasure.

SP: During the 1990's the Triads were racketeering and throughout Hong Kong including the film industry. Do you and Sammo have had any issues with the Triads?

RS: Of course, at that time there was heavy pressure in the Film Business from Triads but no one and I mean no one dared to try anything with Sammo. Especially since he had the black bodyguard from America! LOL! I had the honor to know and learn traditional customs from Sammo Hung's mother about the Chinese culture. She fixed us dinner every night and she was the best cook. Even when I went anywhere in Hong Kong I was aware of the respectful way to operate.

SP: Sammo is one of the original and most successful martial artists; creating and starring in the classics that will last forever. My favorite is Warriors Two followed by Encounters of a Spooky Kind and SPL plus more.

As you lived with Sammo, you must have got to know him. What is Sammo like as an actual person?

RS: I'm glad you ask this question. I never really get asked about Sammo the person. I will say this he is probably the kindest loving and caring person I ever knew. He loves his family more than anything. Look at what he did for me that is the best example to share, a young black kid from the hood with dreams of doing action films. He not only gave me opportunities but loved me enough to let me live with him.

Over the years there have been people that were jealous of my relationship with him at that time. I will save that chapter for my book coming out next year. No matter what the future holds Sammo will always be my teacher, not just of martial arts, but how to treat people with kindness.

SP: Can you please paint a picture of

what Sammo's home and the local area was like? Was it in the city or countryside?

RS: At that time we lived in Kowloon City. It was a beautiful part of Hong Kong. Quite enough to enjoy and raise a family.

SP: What did you guys do on in your free time away from training and films? Did you listen to music, watch TV, SEGA Genesis, go out for dinner, beers and takeaway?

What was it like just hanging out?

RS: Funny thing at the time NYPD Blue was a popular show in the U.S. Sammo loved the way the show was filmed and how the characters were developed. That show was a motivating factor to "Don't Give a Damn" the second film I did for Bojon Films. We spent time playing soccer. We traveled to China for many events. Sammo always had interviews to do or guest appearances on T.V. shows. We went out to his nightclub "TakeOne", a popular place in Hong Kong. Cory Yuen would come and drink with us sometime.

SP: Did Sammo ever talk to you about what his most favorite roles have been?

RS: Yes when he played his Sifu in "Painted Faces" and "Eastern Condors". He loved old war movies like the Dirty Dozen. That film inspired Eastern Condors.

SP: What kind of TV/films does Sammo like and what influences him?

RS: He loves comedies, action films from the U.S. Sammo started using CGI and he was incorporating it in his films moving forward

SP: Did Sammo ever tell you any stories about Enter the Dragon or Bruce Lee that you can tell us?

RS: Yes. He told me when he first met Bruce Lee at Golden Harvest Studios Bruce introduced himself. He said Bruce liked to test people to see where he was on the skill level. At the time Sammo was doing action design for films and had a pretty good reputation. I remember Sammo saying Bruce wanted a friendly test of skills. Sammo said before he could strike Bruce had made contact several times. He said he was one of the fastest he had ever seen. They had so much respect for each other.

I remember Sammo saying he was in a restaurant when he got the news Bruce Lee had passed. He was devastated. Sammo had so much respect and admiration for Bruce Lee. You can see in his performances and the films he's done to show respect for the amazing fighting skills Bruce Lee demonstrated. Enter the Fat Dragon among other performances in his films. My Big Brother Mark Houghton & Sammo recreated the fight between Bruce and Chuck Norris in Way of the Dragon.

SP: 1995 was an eventful year. Firstly, you starred with Sammo & Yuen Biao in "Don't Give a Damn" what it like working with these guys again?

RS: That year was a peak year for me. Getting to work with Sammo & Yuen Biao again was amazing. Yuen Biao and I always hung out every day in Hong Kong along with my brother Colin Chou. Right after shooting that film I started "The Red Wolf". Then something crazy happened, I got an offer to play a lead in a non-action film by Award Winning director Alfred Cheung King Ting titled "My Mistress, My, Wife". It was the first time an African American had an onscreen romance with an Asian female actress.

SP: Secondly in 1995; you also starred in in "The Red Wolf", directed by Yuen-Woo Ping, You also moved out from Sammo's. What was it like at this time?

RS: Working for Yuen Woo Ping was a dream come true. He is the Godfather of Sammo's children. Sammo said he wanted me to meet someone. Next thing you know I'm performing for Yuen Woo Ping. Sammo said he wanted to use me and G-7, a western stunt group I formed in Hong Kong. The film was titled "The Red Wolf".

Yuen Woo Ping is another master filmmaker. The experience is one I will cherish forever. Let me say this, the only reason I got to work with Yuen Woo Ping is because Sammo gave his blessing. I followed Hung Ga Ban, Sammo's group, and that was where my loyalty was always.

SP: What made your decision to move back to the USA?

RS: I remember we were at the airport picking up his son. He asked me what did I want to do with my life .1997 was fast approaching and the film business in Hong Kong had started to slow down tremendously. Most of the projects were starting to be filmed in Mainland China.

He said "I've given you the tools to continue in the film business". He didn't want me to stay in Hong Kong. It was then I made a decision to return to the United States and continue my career in the film industry. Once I returned to the United States, I didn't realize that a lot of my films were being seen on the underground scene here in. So I started getting a lot of offers to do music videos, action directing and eventually directing films. Nothing could have happened if it were not for Sammo. Until the day I leave this Earth I will love him with all my heart.

SP: Do you still keep in contact with Sammo and his family?

RS: Yes when the opportunity presents itself. I have a career in the U.S now as a director and that would not have happened if it were not for Sammo. He's in Shanghai now and with the current restrictions on travel, it's difficult.

SP: What are the most important lessons you have learned from Sammo?

RS: The most important lesson I learned from him is to always treat people with kindness and compassion. He gave me, a black kid from the ghetto, the greatest gift I could have ever asked for. I will always Love Sammo and his family. They are the reason I have everything.

SP: Thank you Bobby for talking the time to talk with us and I am sure we'll again speak soon. Please pass Sammo all our love and respect from Eastern Heroes magazine.

SERVED WITH A SIDE OF SAMMO!

By Jason McNeil

Show-hopping Crossovers with Sammo, Chuck Norris... and a weird magical cat

Twice during its two season run, the ABC Network decided to roll out "crossover episodes" between Martial Law and a couple of its other hit programs, presumably to both tempt viewers to check out what was screening on different nights, as well as just relishing the chance to spread the magical seeds of Sammo across the fields of their various and sundry prime time offerings. (I mean, who wouldn't want a little Sammo Hung on their show?)

First in season one, Sammo Law paid a visit to the windy city of Chicago as a guest star on the mystery/adventure/comedy/supernatural/weird cat show, Early Edition. In season two, Sammo joined forces with none other than CHUCK NORRIS in a two episode crossover with Walker: Texas Ranger!!!

For reasons that will become clear in a moment, let's take a quick look at the second one first, then we'll come back to "magical prophesy cats" in Chicago.....

Walker: Texas Ranger

C'mon, this is a no-brainer! If your network has got a prime time show starring Sammo Hung AND a prime time show starring Chuck Norris, THEY HAVE TO TEAM UP!

I mean, seriously - why would you not?

Starting with Martial Law Season 2, Episode 16, titled "Honor Among Strangers" then hopping from the mean streets of Los Angeles to the dirt roads (OK, some of them are paved) of Texas in Walker: Texas Ranger Season 8, Episode 17, titled "The Day of Cleansing," Sammo and Chuck join forces to take down a group of white supremacist domestic terrorists, who plan to blow up multiple public buildings to launch their "Take Back America for White People" race war.

Both episodes, taken together, are EXCELLENT – far better than they needed to be. I'll admit that, going into this, I was just looking forward to seeing Sammo and Chuck throwing fists and feet, hopefully with each of them pulling out all their best moves to try to "out fu" the other. What we got, though, is a compelling, suspenseful and at times even poignant story about the dangers

of bigots with military grade weapons, and the very real threat of domestic terrorism. Mind you, this was the 1990s, and for an American audience, the memory of "white nationalist" Timothy McVeigh blowing up the Oklahoma City Federal Building was still very fresh in their minds. What could have been nothing more than a very satisfying prime time chop socky fest actually delivered a powerful two episodes that, taken together, clock in at 88 minutes – essentially a full length movie - about a Chinese cop and a Cowboy cop joining forces to kick the shit out of a bunch of militant racists. Good Stuff.

Before moving on, I should mention the damned fine showing by David Keith as the bigoted would-be bomber. Generally, one thinks of Keith as "casting couldn't

get Anthony De Longis, but didn't want to go 'Full Brett Baxter Clark' so this guy's a good way to split the difference" but here he turns in a positively Emmy-worthy

performance as the smug, arrogant, terrifying baddie that both flirts a little with Bond Villain-ness but, also, is "real" enough to remind you (very uncomfortably) of your racist uncle holding forth about "the blacks" after his fourth cup of Christmas nog.
OK, all that having been said – the Martial Law/Walker: Texas Ranger crossover is AMAZING! Definitely give it a watch! Now we come back to the aforementioned crossover with ABC's hard-to-define action-mystery-supernatural series, Early Edition.

Early Edition

Where to begin? Having never seen this show before, I was at a bit of a loss to figure out what, exactly, was going on. (I watched it as a one-off, with no context, as a "Bonus Feature" of the Martial Law Complete Series DVD Boxed Set. BTW, both of the aforementioned Walker eps are on there, too!)

The short version is that there's a sort of bumbling, stumbling, low rent 90s version of Dick Van Dyke trying unsuccessfully to channel a bit of Jim Carrey-ness, who, for reasons that are not explained, gets a copy of tomorrow's newspaper today, delivered to his door every morning by a presumably magical cat. He then runs around the rest of the episode trying to stop all the bad things that he reads about in the "tomorrow paper" from happening today. Also, he may or may not own a bar, which is tended by "single mom with an annoying kid" Kristy Swanson, who was presumably cursing every day she had to plow through this incomprehensible plot muddle while Sarah Michelle Gellar was absolutely KILLING IT on another network as "Buffy the Vampire Slayer" - a role that Ms. Swanson originated on the big screen just a few years earlier, to zero fanfare. But, I digress.....

So, there's something about a stolen helmet and some muggings and Chinese smugglers and an annoying lady who is a bad artist but also her uncle who isn't really her uncle but it turns out is her uncle after all, who Sammo catches then doesn't arrest, because of a bullet and something about his mom being an archaeologist......

OK, everything else aside, WHAT'S WITH THE MAGICAL CAT?

Where does the cat come from? Is it a ghost cat? SINCE WHEN DO CATS EVEN FETCH THE PAPER? That's a "dog thing." Cats just sit on the sofa and look smug, then start meowing up a storm whenever you open a can of tuna.

Try as I might, and even with multiple re-watches, I couldn't figure the show out and I couldn't get past the damned magical, newspaper delivering, future predicting, possibly angelic or demonic cat.

So I decided to go straight to the source and hopefully get the answers I so desperately need to figure out just what the hell is going on with Early Edition.

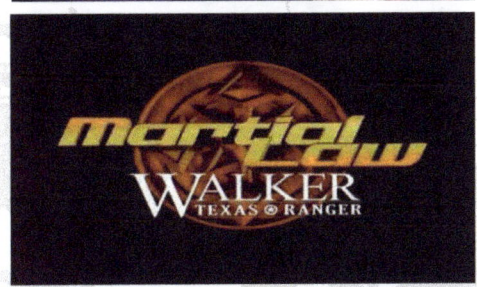

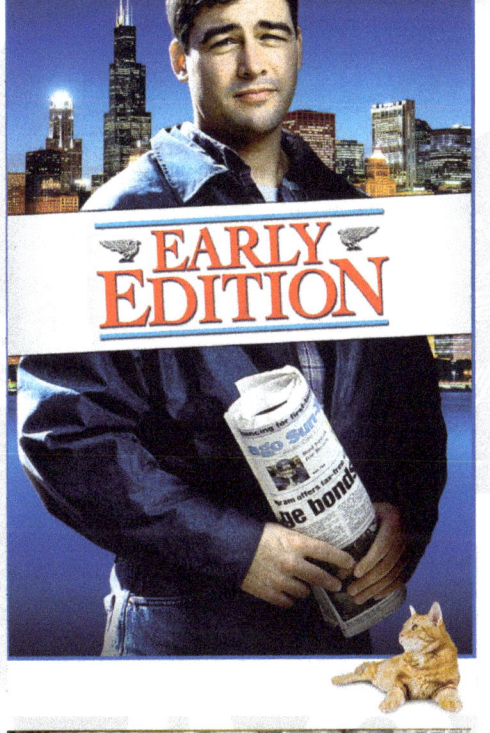

around the apartment. I just picked one up one day – probably 1998-ish – and whoa! I was hooked!"

EH: "Damn! That's nice to hear!"

Panther: "I mean, I've been buying the new ones on Amazon but, you know, if Kung-Fu Ricky wants to throw a puss a free subscription, I wouldn't say no..... (laughs)"

EH: (laughing as well) "OK, I'll pass that along!"

Panther: "Hey, hey... I'm just sayin....."

EH: "So, wait..... You mentioned Katie."

Panther: "Yeah."

EH: "That was Katie, as in Katie the Capuchin monkey who played 'Marcel' on the first season of Friends?"

Panther: "The one and only. Yeah, Katie and I were pretty tight back in the day. We were both repped out of Hollywood Animals in Santa Clarita, and we just kept... I mean, obviously we weren't going to the same auditions – I mean, hello! Monkey, cat, right? But we kept crossing paths and we both got cast in big hit TV series at the same time – we were essentially the top stars at Hollywood Animals mid-to-late 90s – so we kept ending up at the same parties and stuff and, lo and behold, we became besties! We had some pretty wild times – probably peaked around when she got cast in that Dustin Hoffman movie, Outbreak. We were actually sharing an apartment a block off the Sunset at the time and,,, whew! Between the two of us, I think we got petted and got our bellies scratched by every groupie on the Strip!"

EH: "Fascinating! And – damn – there's a million questions I'd like to ask you about the Hollywood party days...."

Panther: "And I'd be happy to tell you all about the parts I can remember...."

EH: "But what I really need you to tell me about is Early Edition...."

Panther: "OK"

EH: "Because – OK, admittedly, I only watched the one episode – the crossover with Martial Law and, frankly, I couldn't make heads or tails of it."

Panther: "Yeahhhhh, that was a weird one. When I first heard that they were bringing Sammo Hung for a crossover, I told the show-runner 'This doesn't make any sense.' I mean, the whole point is that Gary – the protagonist – is supposed to be this completely average, normal guy who has to overcome impossible odds. He's like the audience's avatar, you know? So they can see themselves in the "What would I do if an otherworldly cat brought me tomorrow's newspaper and all of a sudden I had to beat the bad guys and save people's lives?' Instead, you bring in Sammo Hung, who's this badass bonafide kung-fu master, and he just sort of plows thru the bad guys like "all you can eat" chop suey, while Gary just stands around getting coffee and accidentally buys an antique helmet as part of an ugly sculpture.... It just didn't make any sense."

EH: "Yeah, Gary seemed almost like…."

Panther: "Like a background character in his own show, right?"

EH: "Exactly!"

Panther: "Yeah, Sammo was a great guy to work with and I'll always be proud to say I shared the screen with him, but that crossover just didn't work. NOT my favorite episode."

EH: "So, I've got to ask: What exactly was Carl the Cat? I mean, was he an angel, or just an otherworldly delivery feline, or…. I mean, forgive me for saying this, but isn't fetching the paper normally a 'dog thing?'"

Panther: "Traditionally, yes it is. You don't normally see cats fetching anything. We'll chase a dollar store laser pointer all day, but as far as going out to get the newspaper.... hell, we're more likely to either piss on it or shred it with our claws. Or maybe even both."

EH: "Yeah, you don't see a lot of people in the park, throwing sticks to play 'fetch' with their tabbys."

Panther: "Exactly. Throw a stick and tell a cat "Fetch, boy!' and we're just going to sit there and look at you like you're stupid. (laughs) I call it Kitty Judge-y Face. We're great at that."

EH: "So… why then a cat who delivers prophesy in the form of a morning newspaper?"

Panther: "You know, I wish I could say something about how the network was trying to 'be more inclusive' or 'throw off species stereotypes' or something like that. I really would! But frankly... (pauses and licks his butthole for a full 30 seconds, then resumes) Sorry, what was I saying?"

EH: "Something about stereotypes."

Panther: "Oh, yeah. Right, As I was saying, I'd love to chalk it up to some noble or even artistic license, but the fact is that I haven't got the first fekking idea why they picked a cat instead of a dog to fetch the magic paper, To me, at first, I was a struggling animal actor and it was just a job. I would've been thrilled at that point just to score a Meow Mix commerical! Then it was a 'recurring role.' Then it was a starring role on a hit TV show! I didn't ask too many questions, besides 'How many pages do I have this week?' and 'How much am I getting paid?' I mean, I think I had some stock answer at the time – probably just repeating something I heard in acting class – about how Carl was a manifestation of Gary's subconscious. How he's too insecure to fully accept his own incredible power of prophesy, so his subconscious creates a cat to serve as the vehicle for his gift. And he naturally would choose a cat because a dog would be too quote unquote friendly, while a cat would be more aloof, allowing him to distance himself from the frightening enormity of both his gift and the responsibility that gift has burdened him with. Something like that."

EH: "Wow."

Panther: "Yeahhhhh, but that's a bunch of bullshit. (laughs) I was doing a LOT of catnip back then, and that was probably just me talking high! (vigorously scratches behind ear with his left paw.)

EH: "So even you, who played it on TV, don't have an answer to 'What the hell is up with the mysterious cat who delivers the magical newspaper in Early Edition?'"

Panther: "You know, as I recall, Sammo had a line in that episode that summed it up perfectly. When Gary was fumbling around trying to explain what was going on, Sammo stopped him and said: 'Some things can be explained. Some things simply are.' I'm just gonna leave it at that."

About the author: Jason McNeil is an actor, writer and martial artist, who can't help but wonder why anyone who got tomorrow's newspaper today wouldn't skip the headlines and go straight to the stock report while calling his broker.....

COMING SOON
SPECIAL HARDBACK SAMMO HUNG EDITION

ENTER THE *Legend*

Enter the Dragon opening sequence. By Rick Baker

In 1974 I went to the cinema to get my first glimpse of Bruce Lee on the big screen. Little did I realise at the time I would also be introduced to many other stars that would become a staple diet of my cinema/video watching in the years to come. Jim Kelly, Bolo Yeung, Angela Mao and of course Sammo Hung (I did not even know who Jackie Chan was in 1974 so his cameo would have meant nothing to me)

The first scene shown in the movie was actually the last scene Bruce filmed for the movie. Bruce is fighting a young Sammo Hung. The scene took two days to film in April, 1973. Bruce Lee also directed this opening scene with his own film crew as the Warner's crew had left Hong Kong by this time! Although Sammos time on screen is short, the opening scene was impacting to a young boy watching his first bonafidee Bruce Lee Kung Fu movie.

As I write this, it so happens to be the day Bruce Lee past 20.07.1973, I re-watch the scene and reflect that shortly after shooting the scene, Bruce Lee would pass away making this the last time he would be in front of the camera. However his opponent (Sammo Hung) his career is just beginning, and he would become one of the most influential people in Hong Kong Cinema both acting on screen, his ground breaking fight choreography and his keen eye for directing. Bruce Obviously had an eye for talent! Luckily the huge gap he left after his passing was to be filled by some of those starting their career in his last movie. Sammo hung played a big part in that along with Jackie Chan who continued to grow the Golden harvest stable, and Hong Kong cinema was to be secured for the future. So when you watch that opening scene i like to think that Bruce was passing the baton on to a very worthy opponent carrying the touch of Bruce lee's legacy for many decades to come.

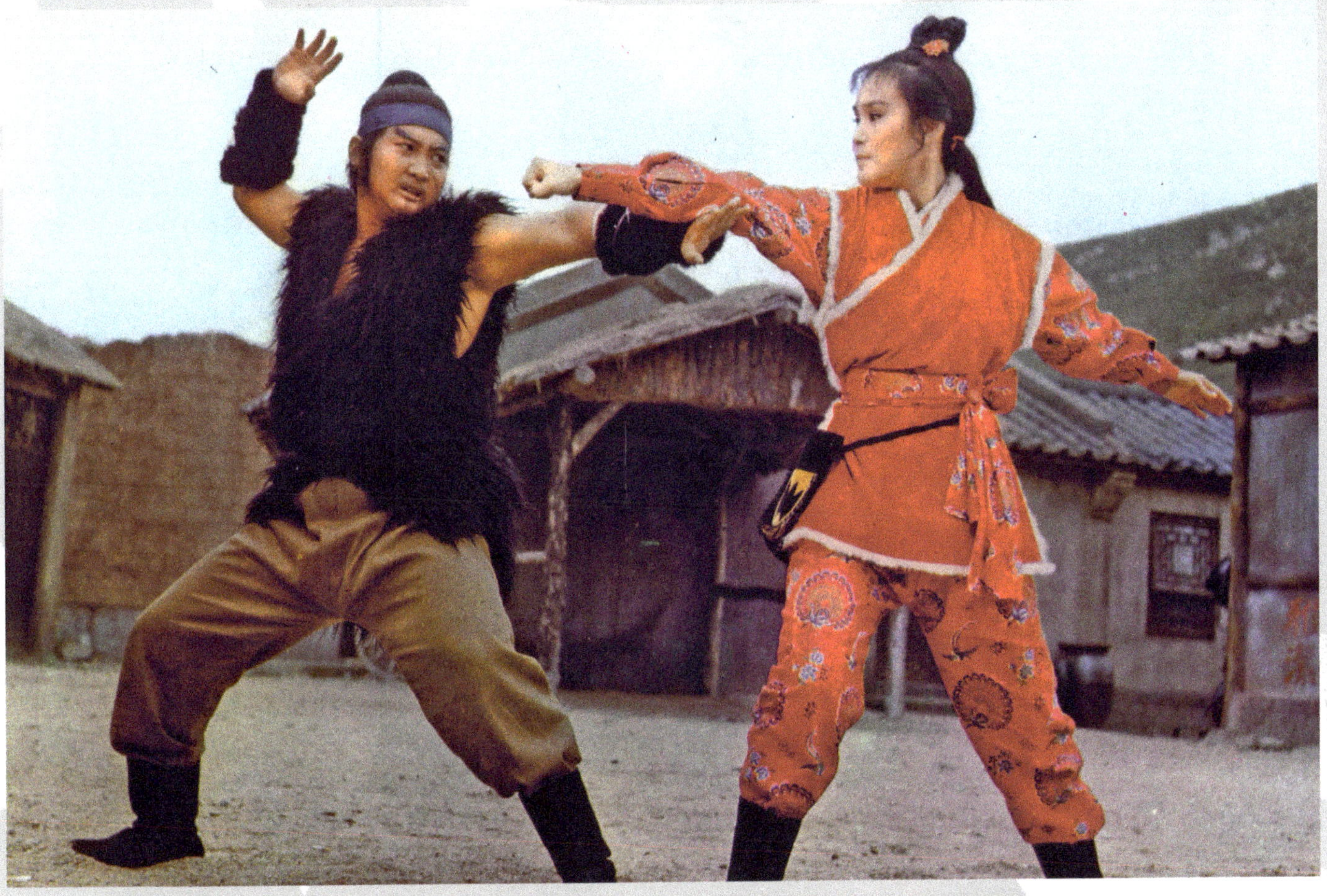

袁和平 關德興 樊梅生 鍾發
元彪 李海生 馮克安
洪金寶 韋白 陳琪琪 唐晶 蔣金
仁者無敵
鄒文懷

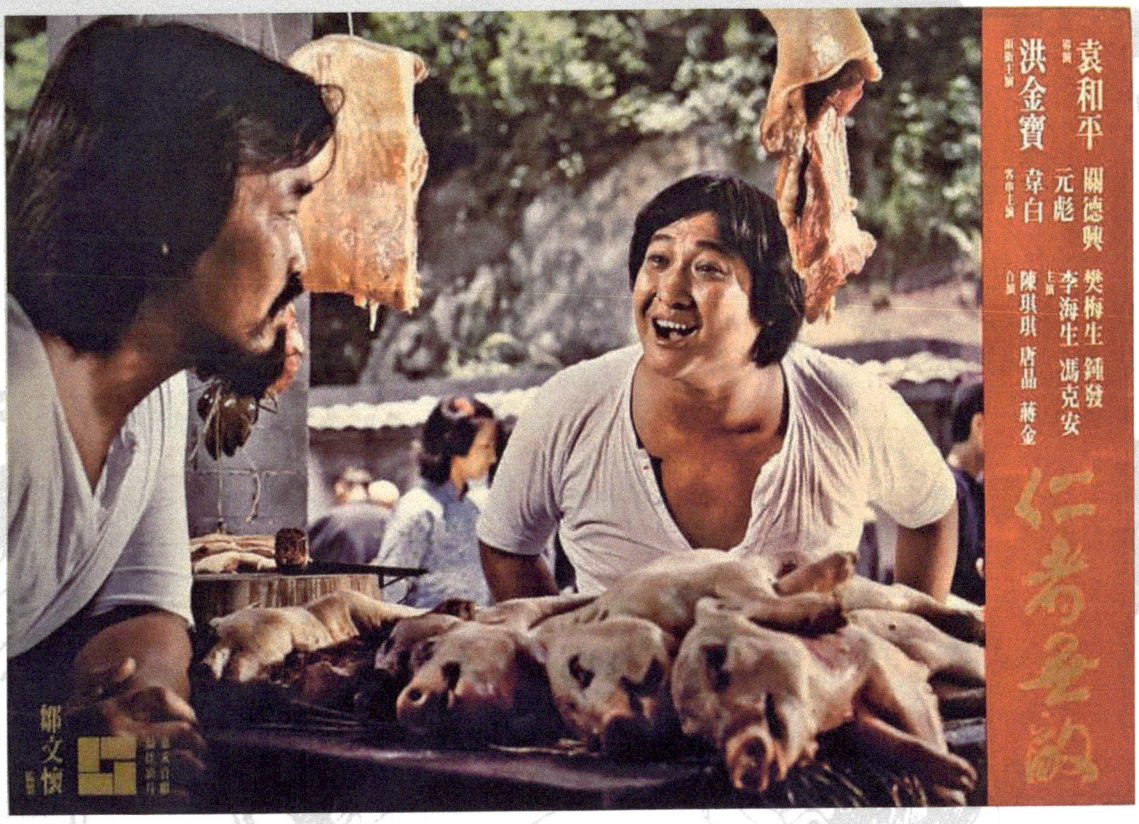

Page 77   Eastern Heroes Sammo Hung Special

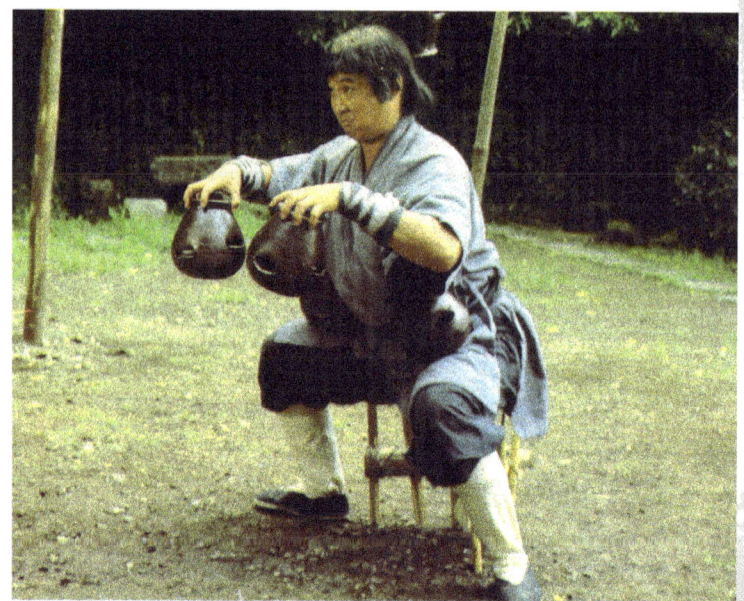

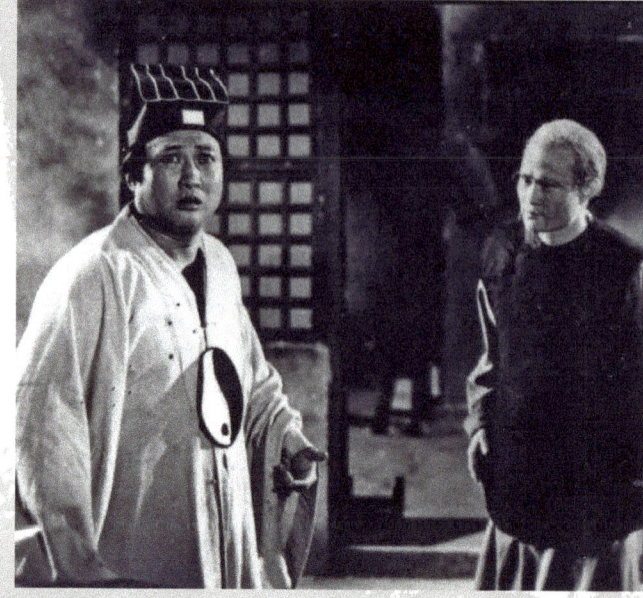

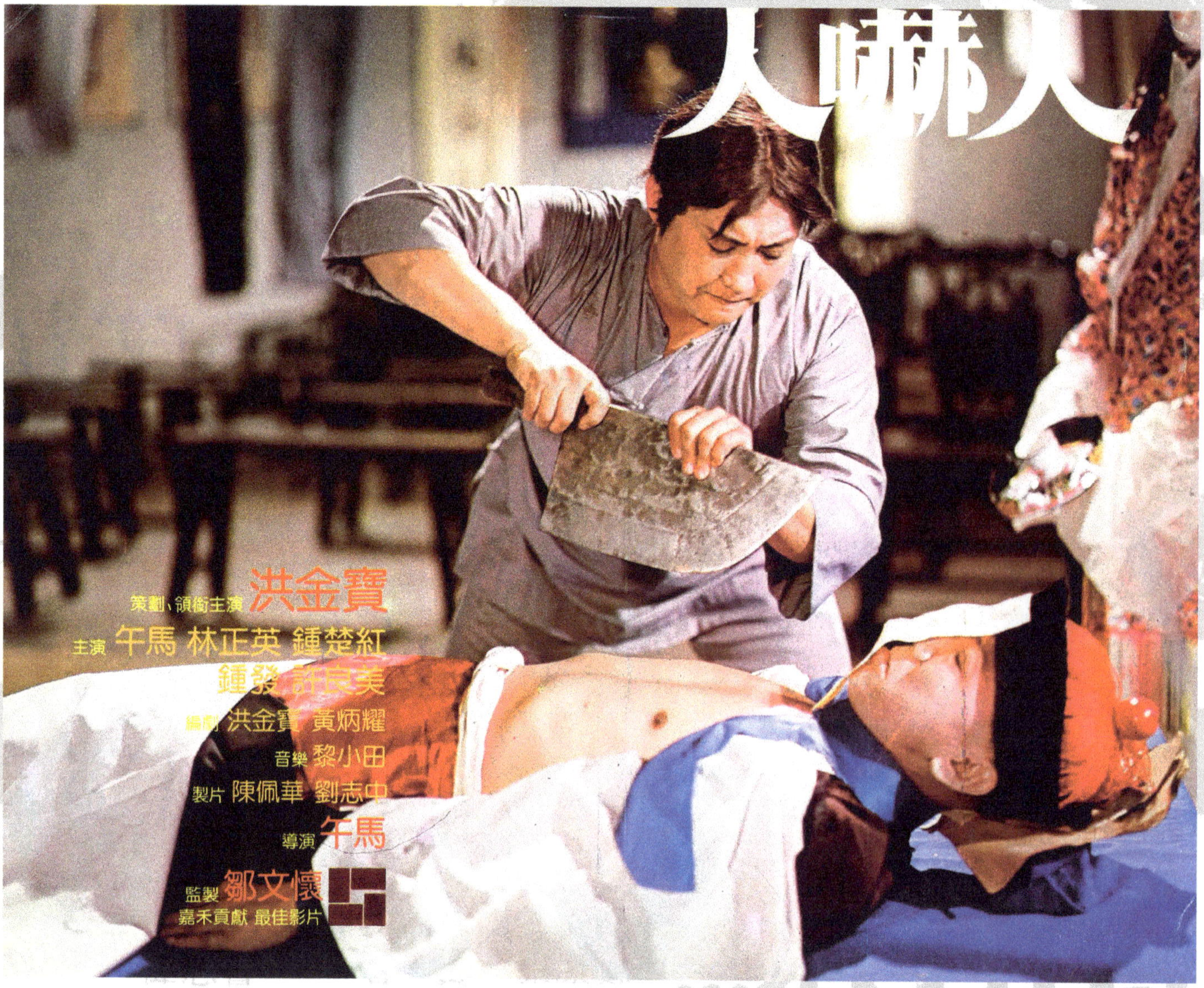

人嚇人
策劃、領銜主演 洪金寶
主演 午馬 林正英 鍾楚紅
鍾發 許良美
編劇 洪金寶 黃炳耀
音樂 黎小田
製片 陳佩華 劉志中
導演 午馬
監製 鄒文懷
嘉禾貢獻 最佳影片

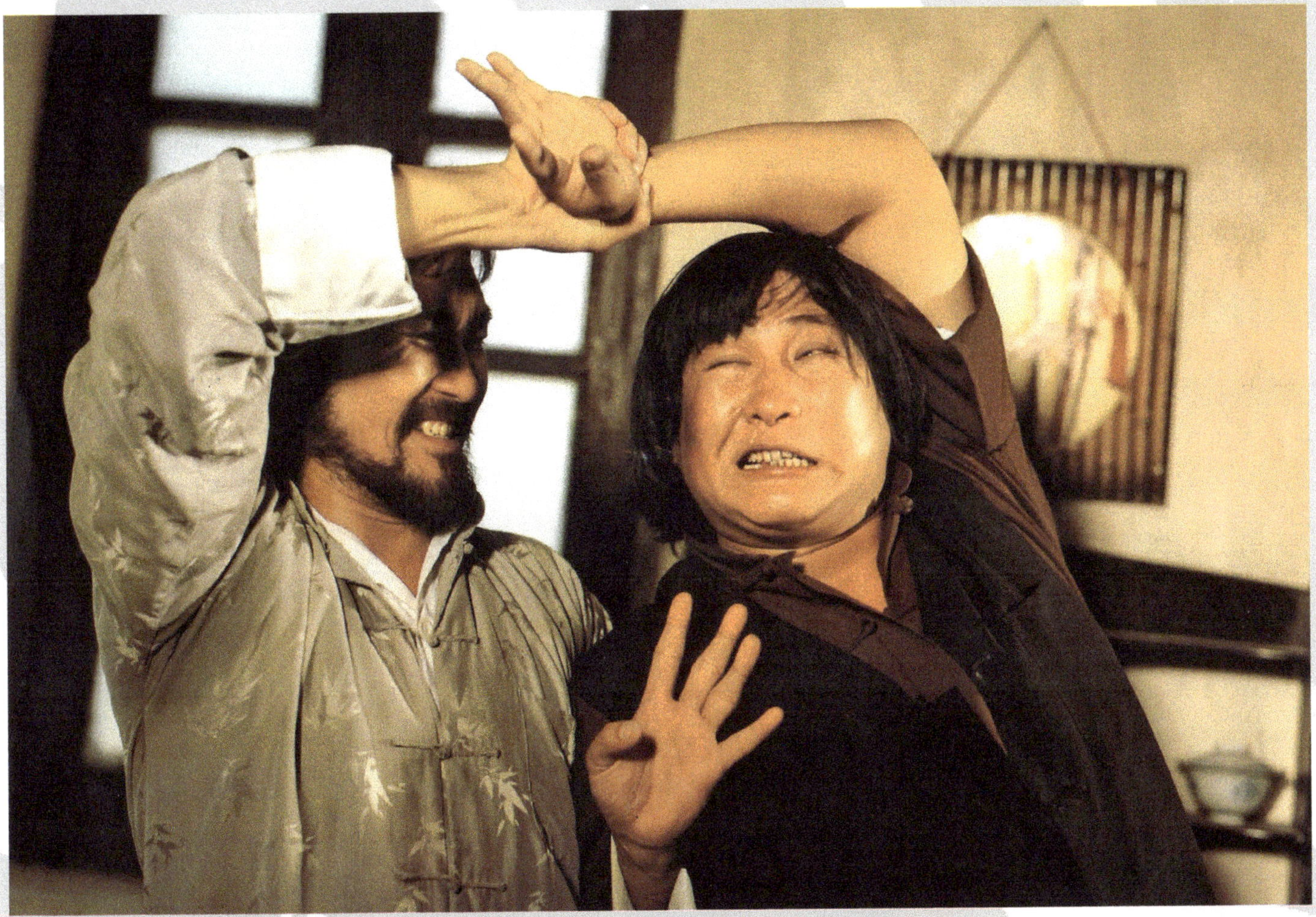

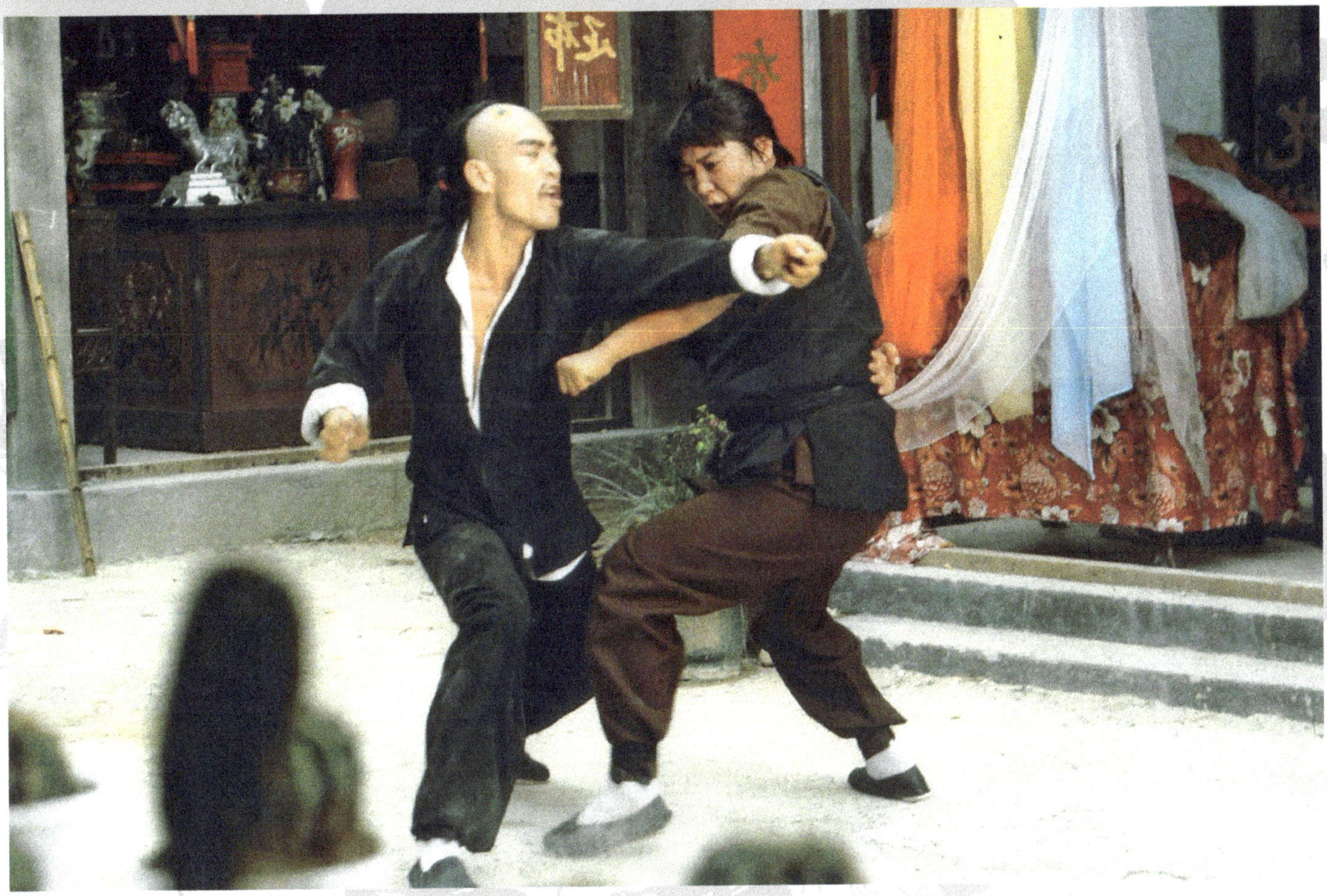

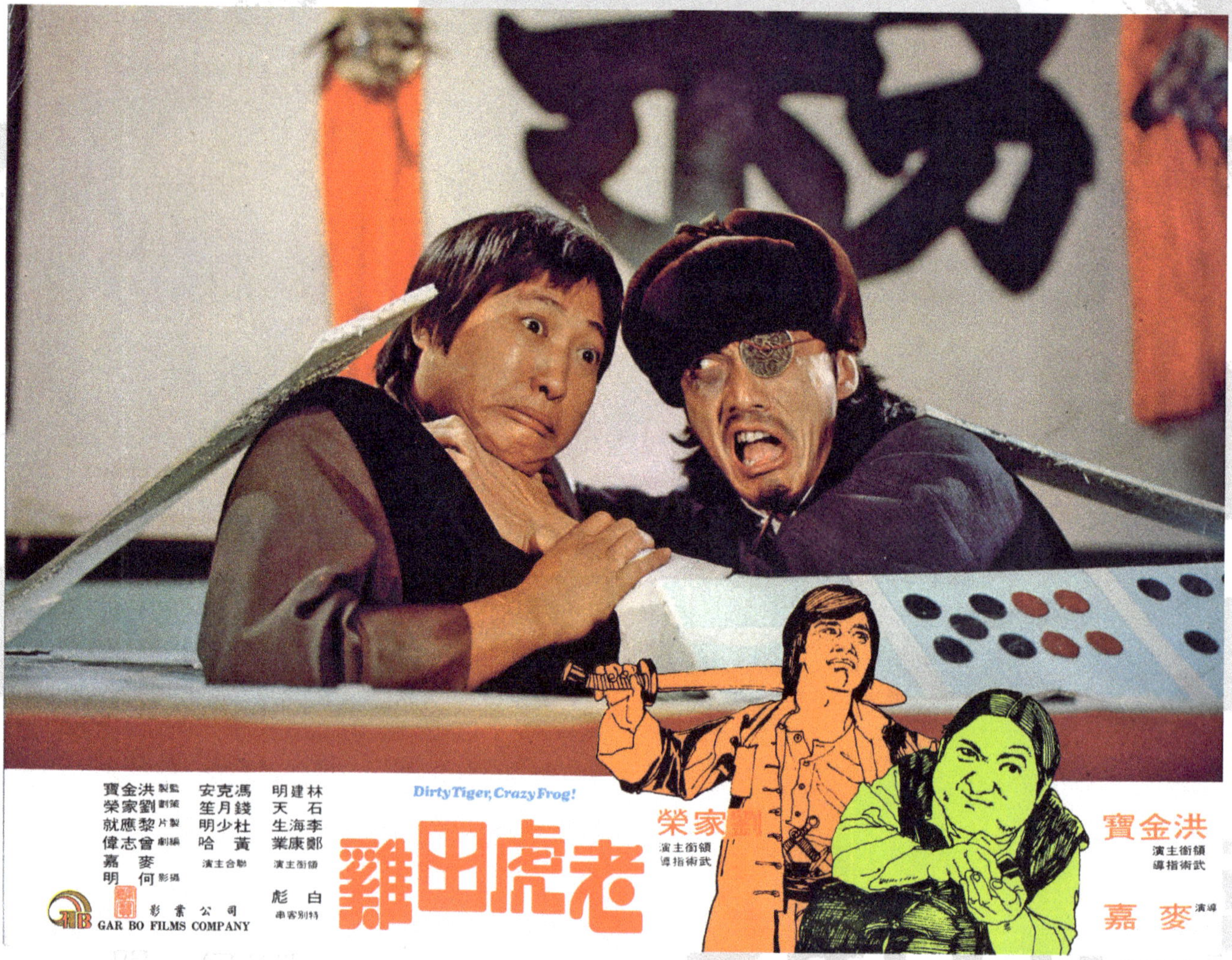

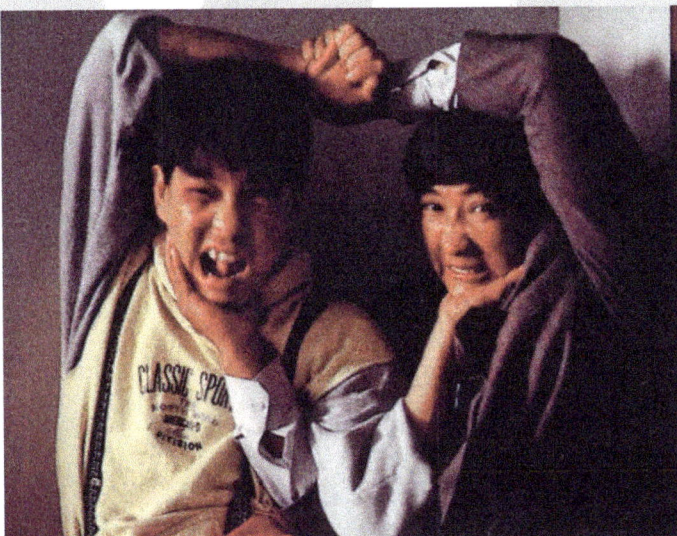

DRAGONS FOREVER

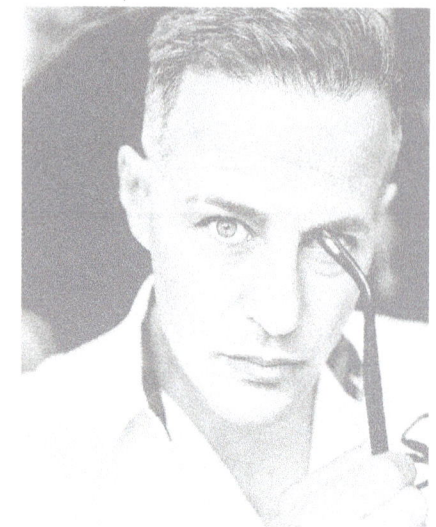

Louis MANDYLOR
Interview by Rick Baker

Louis Mandylor. Is an Australian actor, writer and director.
Louis is also one of the nicest guys I have ever had the pleasure of interviewing. Smart and pin Sharpe focused on his future and career. He kindly took time out of his busy schedule to talk about his career and the respect he had for Sammo Hung whilst working on "Martial Law"

RB: Did you get swept up in the martial arts craze of the 1970s?

LM: Of course, yeah. Who wasn't? Bruce Lee was the centre of that movement, end of story. I've been really lucky since then to meet and work with people who were close with him and worked with him. Sammo Hung in Martial Law, and Jackie Chan and that whole action crew. Ron Balicki is a dear friend of mine. He's married to Diana Lee Inosanto, the daughter of Dan Inosanto, who was the right-hand man of Bruce Lee. He taught Bruce the nunchaku routine for Enter the Dragon. So yeah, I got swept away in it all like every other kid.

RB: Did you actually join a club?

LM: I did. I started karate before I started boxing and kickboxing. A style called Goju Kai. Primarily it was just to get out of double English. It had that hard, rigid style. I was an avid fight fan. My father used to watch all the Ali/Frazier fights, so it was a big part of my life. I took up boxing, which seemed the real deal. To be brutally honest, over the years I've beaten a lot of martial artists. When your goal is to knock someone unconscious as quickly as possible, it's different to all those unnecessary movements. Boxing and Thai kickboxing became my Bible. The funny thing is, when I got to Hollywood the last thing I wanted to do was any action movies. I just wanted to act! Maybe, looking back, it's a mistake. I should have done what Scott did, and said 'I'm going to do this action thing and do it better than anyone on the planet.' Which Scott does? That's why he's Number One. But me? I was different. I wanted to

learn the craft. The way I segued into the business was almost by chance. I went to LA to pursue a professional boxing career, and I was really close to getting a contract.

RB: Wow!

LM: At the same time, I was sitting in my brother's acting class. I had these two worlds rubbing up against each other. At some point they came together. Through the boxing I got the chance to do a movie called Necessary Roughness. It's a canny story. I had been on a one-way ticket, aiming to be a world champion. I was training every day, I fought in almost every gym in Los Angeles, I fought every young fighter in Los Angeles, and I was ready. Then I went to a party and met Mindy Marin. She asked, 'Are you an actor?' And I lied! I said yes. She gave me a piece of paper. It was a monologue to audition for Stanley Dragoti at Paramount Pictures on a Monday morning. However, I also had my contract for a sparring session on Sunday against a guy called The Fixer. So, I did eight rounds with The Fixer, where we kicked each other's heads in, basically. On Monday morning I looked quite beaten up, but went in and gave probably the best audition I've ever done. I was so beaten up that I underplayed everything! I got contracts for the fight AND the film! That's when my life changed. I had to make a decision. I chose the acting.

RB: It's interesting, because at that stage, the action stuff with Stallone and Van Damme was big news. Scott said to me recently that he was born ten years too late. That if he'd been around in the 80s and 90s, he'd have been huge. With people like Cynthia Rothrock, there was a market back then.

LM: Right. But at that time, I had people in my ear going, 'We can make you a movie star, you can act, focus on the craft.' In any case, it is what it is. The irony is that at the age of 50-plus, I'm starting to do some kick-ass action films. People are starting to realise that I can act, and deliver.

RB: Nowadays, there's no ageism with some of the action films coming out. The Expendables, Taken, Nobody. There's a swing towards older action stars. Although, I think you made the right choice at the start. There's a longer career in acting than there is damaging yourself doing stunts.

LM: Yeah, and the problem is, lots of action films have a garbage story. That's what kills the actors. You've got some great actors and they're stuck with bad characterisation and cliches. Then sometimes you'll get someone who can mix action with a decent story with decent characters. When you can do that, then, yeah, you've got something beautiful.

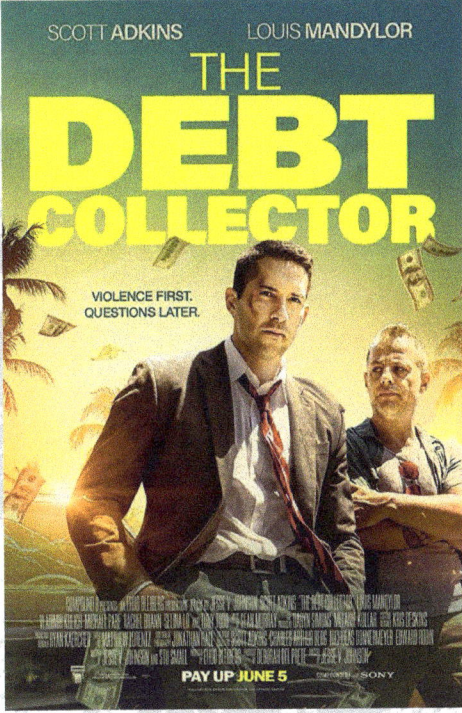

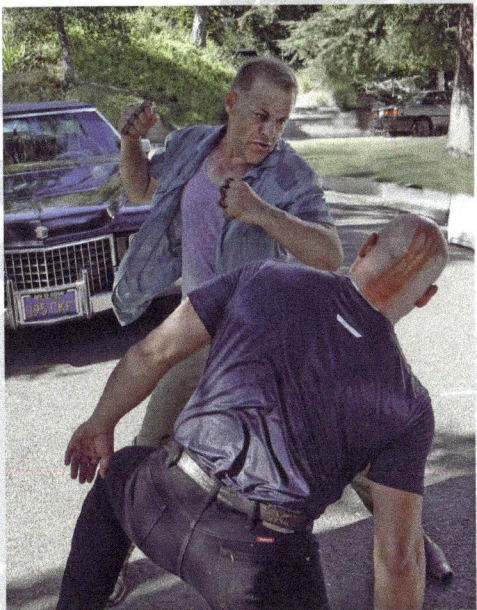

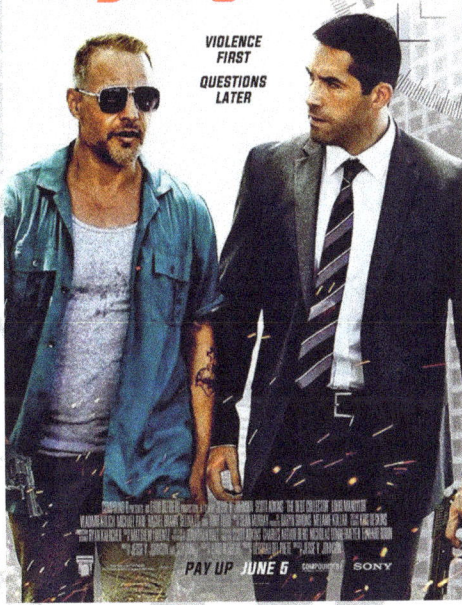

Personally, that's why I think the Debt Collectors films have a cult following. Jesse is an amazing human being and a dear friend. When I read that script, I saw that it had heart and character. Realistically, it wasn't about the action, even though it was an action film. It was about two lost souls who have no life. I loved that. The investment in the characters gives the action meaning.

He's one of the three gems – him, Jackie and Jet. Sammo was one of the hardest men I've met. He's not just an actor who knows martial arts.

RB: I did a video interview with him in the 90s and he spoke pretty good English. But I guess it's different when it's lines? Kelly mentioned that he had an earpiece and they fed him his lines?

LM: Yeah, they did for a bit, but after that he was fine. He caught on quick. That didn't matter, though. He used to just kick

spin back and do everything. We had Andy Cheng, who's a dear friend and one of the best directors of stuntmen in the world. That guy has visions like no one can even imagine. He's great.

RB: I love Andy!

LM: I remember the pilot. The first time I worked with these guys. I did my first fight scene with the stuntmen that Andy brought over. The Americans on that show kept getting fired! Only the best survived. During the scene they did actually hit me full contact. They hit me in the head, the body, bitch-slapped me, then kicked me in the face. Not hard, but I remember thinking, 'What just happened?' They said, 'That's how we do it.' I had to make a decision within two seconds: do I complain and be this dude whose like, 'Hey man, we don't touch each other here', or go with it. So I thought, you know what, I'm a street kid, so let's go with it. Stuntmen were asked to leave because they wouldn't go with it. The level of the action was so high - it was incredible.

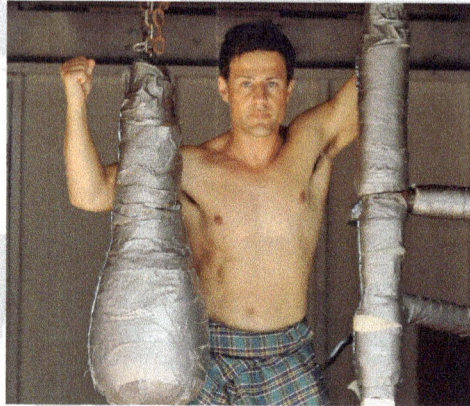

everyone's ass, and boy, could he!

RB: Sammo didn't think he'd make it in America, but after Rush Hour and Rumble in the Bronx, it maybe gave him the confidence to try? He was a large man, but with his Peking Opera training, he could perform.

LM: Yeah, he's about my height, maybe a little taller, but he's a heavy guy. Then they'd say, 'Action!' and he would flip and kick and

RB: Did Sammo do choreography?

LM: No, they had a bunch of guys there doing all that. Andy Cheng wore a fat suit to look like Sammo. They did a bit where there was a moving limousine, and Sammo's character had to sprint and jump feet-first

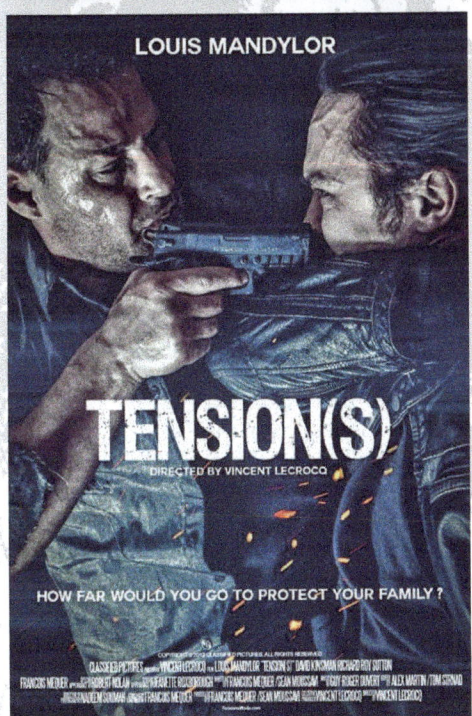

through the open passenger window. One mistake on that and you're finished! I saw them do that and thought, wow, this is how they do it over there. I saw them do break-falls from 15 feet onto concrete with nothing. One actor asked for an armadillo and Stanley Tong, the director, said, 'You don't need one, you're only coming off a bench.' The guy insisted that he needed one because there wasn't enough room. Tong took off his earphones, climbed up, did a backflip, just like that, in his t-shirt, landed on his back, got up and said, 'Can you do it? No? Go.'

They got someone else, just like that. That was the energy on that show, and why the first season was so fantastic and successful. They brought a new level to US television. They made changes later in the year, and I don't know why. They had magic in a bottle. I asked to leave at the end of the year. It felt like they were trying to do a Rush Hour rip off. Why? The show was a hit. Rush Hour had its own magic – don't try and rip it off. We had a great show. Just make it better. Build the characters, do the action. It was new. The American audience was eating it up. I didn't like this new direction. I asked whether or not I was needed. They said maybe not. So I said thanks, and left. I was sad because I loved the show, I just knew they were making bad decisions. I said that the show would be gone in six months, and it was. That show should have run for five/six years.

RB: Did the exposure stand you in good stead?

LM: Yeah, your stock goes up. I left at the right time to retain credibility.

RB: Any stories about you and Sammo?

LM: Sammo was really distant for the first couple of weeks, from everyone. Obviously! He'd been royalty in Hong Kong, and now he was in America and it was a different culture and language. I stood off him for a bit because I didn't want to add to the pressure. It was a gradual friendship. I love conversation and jokes, and he warmed up to me. We became kinda pals. I think it was on racetrack episode that things changed. We were filming a really serious scene where we're interrogating this dude who's the murderer. I remember leaning over to my stunt double and saying, 'I think I'm going to break the ice today.' He asked what I was going to do. I replied: 'I think in the middle of Sammo's dialogue I'm going to stick my finger up his arse.' We were both wearing suits, standing next to each other, doing this scene. The camera was on Sammo Hung, this icon from the other side of the planet, a serious killing machine, and I've decided to 'thumb' him. That's when we bonded! It could have gone south, really bad, but when I did that he screamed, swore, and broke into laughter. Why I did that, I don't know! We became really good friends after that.

RB: Did they leave the scene in, or is it just an outtake?

LM: (laughs) I think it's an outtake! From that moment on, he 'got' me. And I 'got' him. He's a great guy, with a sense of humour. His wife was lovely. The three of us would converse a lot. I had a lot of lunches at their house. It was an honour. The guy's a legend.

RB: Thank you Louis for taking time out to talk to me. And look forward to do a further interview on your new projects that you have in development.

ANDY CHENG
Action Director Extrordinaire
Interview by Rick Baker

Cheng Kai-Chung, also known as Andy Cheng, is a Hong Kong actor, stuntman, choreographer, martial artist, and director. He was a prominent member of the Jackie Chan Stunt Team from the late 1990s to early 2000s until he broke out on his own and became a member of the Stunts Unlimited team.

Andy has become a regular amongst the pages of the magazine, so by popular demand I called him up and asked him if he would pay his respects to his big brother and reflect on his time working on Martial Law. Of course the answer was yes without hesitation!

RB: How did you get the gig on Martial Law?

AC: I met Stanley Tong a long time ago when Jackie had a birthday party. Stanley shared an idea with Andre Morgan, who was a producer on Martial Law. Morgan brought Stanley Tong to America to do a movie – Mr Magoo. They then paired up to produce Martial Law for CBS. They wanted Stephen Chow in the lead, not Sammo Hung. I was a stunt double for Stephen in his last two movies.

RB: Which films were they?

AC: Six Million Dollar Man…

RB: I saw that in Hong Kong! I had the rights to that film for a while!

AC: The other was Love on Delivery. Stanley asked Jackie if he could borrow me after I worked on Who Am I? He wanted me to be Stephen's stunt double on the pilot for Martial Law, and to help with choreography.

RB: Stephen was definitely on-board to do this series?

AC: Yeah! And then he quit, for whatever reason. We were already there prepping. We had to think, ok, what do we do now? Sammo came onto the production right away. But then, we needed a double for him, and we found a bigger guy from America to do that. Before we even finished the pilot, the studio said that they'd pick up the show. Twenty-two episodes. I was only hired for the pilot, but Stanley said to me, 'Why don't you double Sammo?'

RB: In a fat suit?

AC: They gave me a suit to wear, and I filmed the first series. The second series was picked up pretty quickly, but I had to return to the production of Shanghai Noon, so I didn't re-join the tv show. They got an American stunt man to double for Sammo in

the second series. I thought I might return for the third season but they cancelled it!

RB: When I spoke to Sammo in the 1990s, he didn't think he stood a chance of working in America. Brett Ratner thought that after the success of Rush Hour, the gate had opened for Hong Kong actors. So it was good to see Sammo get a chance. What was it like working with him?

AC: It was great! The show was good, Sammo was full of ideas, and it was fun.

RB: Sammo was used to getting involved in direction and things. Did that happen on Martial Law?

AC: Not really. But he judged it! If we came up with an idea, he'd give his input. He'd be like, 'what's this?!' and if he didn't like it, we'd have to think of something else. He made sure he was happy with the choreography. It was a great experience. I'd already worked with him before on Mr Nice Guy, so we already had a good working relationship.

RB: Was it difficult in America, where they have unions and different safety laws? Sammo and Jackie came from the same background, where they could do little tricks to make things work, or whatever. Did Sammo find it difficult working without the freedom he had in Hong Kong?

AC: We found it tough, but we had ways of doing things. In an episode there was maybe 3 days of fight filming and 6 or 7 of drama, so we only had two fights to prepare. The Hong Kong style helped us to prep for whatever we needed. We didn't break the rules, but we'd get things done.

RB: How did Sammo find working on a tv series rather than a movie?

AC: Basically, he had no problem. The toughest thing for him was speaking English. He spent all day learning the dialogue. Physical stuff? No problem. Performing? No problem. The language was the difficult thing.

RB: You'd think that at the end of the series, his English would be very good.

AC: You'd think so! But in season two, it was the same thing. He still had a hard time, and he had to study the dialogue a lot with the writer.

RB: When I met Sammo, I had Toby Russell with me, who spoke Cantonese. People told me that Sammo wouldn't speak to me in English. We sat down, and he spoke English the whole time! His English was quite good!

AC: (laughing) Yeah, he can speak English. Conversational English is different. You can ask if someone understands you, or you can work out if they can't. Dialogue on a script

AC: You have to think, and act, and talk, and pronounce it right. It's not easy, I can tell you that. What Sammo and Jackie does is amazing.

RB: Yuen Biao spoke no English at all.

AC: Those guys are on another level.

RB: You've worked with Jackie and so many people. In your opinion, how do you rate Sammo as an all-round director, actor and choreographer?

AC: High, of course. Legend.

RB: Some people think his contribution to Hong Kong cinema is incredible…

AC: I rate him number one. If you were on set, experiencing what he did. He did choreography for Bruce Lee. He's the real deal.

RB: I've learnt from a few people, like

Mark Houghton, that when he fights, he can really hit you!

AC: Yeah. He's tough! When he was at the top, no one wanted to even touch him. He's still one of the best. It's hard to compare, but he's one of the top five toughest fighters.

RB: He's one of the few people I've met in the business who I've felt that, if you met him down a back alley, would give you a real fight. Forget the movies, he's real-life tough!

AC: On a movie set, when he's in charge, he's the most scary person you'll ever meet!

RB: People say that Sammo is the only person who Jackie doesn't challenge when he is directing him. Is this true?

AC: Of course, he sees him as a master…

RB: Like a big brother?

AC: Yes. He respects him and listens to him one hundred percent.

RB: How do you find him as a person off set?

AC: He's funny! Very direct and a fast thinker. He plays golf. He started me off playing golf! We were shooting Mr Nice Guy and he would go to the driving range for a couple of hours before filming every day.

RB: Is he any good?

AC: Yeah. We played golf during the shooting of Martial Law. His temper! When he had a bad shot, he'd be roaring with anger! He's very competitive.

RB: My friend Toby was on the set of Moon Warriors. He said that when it was lunchtime, the cast and crew would be at the caterers. Sammo would have his own table, cooking his own food!

AC: He does that! He has a lot of energy. He'd play golf, then film, then cook lunch, then film, then cook dinner. During Martial Law he'd call and invite us to his home for food.

RB: He must be a good cook?

AC: Look at his size!

RB: In England, when people saw Sammo Hung, the reason he got so much admiration was because it was expected that fighters were skinny and trim. Then they saw Sammo doing backflips and all sorts. People with a bigger body thought, wow, if that guy can do it… They didn't realise that he'd been training since he was a child. They thought he looked fun and cuddly. A friend of mine trained Sammo for Eastern Condors. Sammo went to his house in Hong Kong and stayed. He told me he had to put a chain around the fridge because at night time Sammo would sneak down and try and raid it! If you watch the film, Sammo is quite slim, and apparently it was very hard to keep it that way.

is different. You're reading words. And you have to combine it with acting.

RB: That's what I figured. It must be so hard to act in another language.

AC: That might be the only moment he's skinny. He loves food! Recently he trimmed down.

RB: I don't know if you've seen him recently, but his health isn't that good.

AC: His health is good, but he has problems with his knees. After so many years of action, with his size, doing things like flipping, his knees have suffered. That's why you've seen him in a wheelchair or with a cane. It's why he's trimmed down, so there's less pressure on his knees.

RB: Years ago, I was sad when I saw Sammo on a tv show and he supposedly had a gambling problem. He was going broke, because he loved the horse racing.

AC: I didn't know. I know he likes his gambling, but I didn't know that. When I'm in Hong Kong, I like to gamble on the horses too! Hong Kong people like to gamble. People can get addicted. I've lost money before in Vegas. One time I lost three months of money in three days. My wife wasn't happy! Never again!

RB: Have you got any stories from Martial Law?

AC: I remember I had to fight against him in one scene. I had two swords. He had two tennis rackets. I tried to block everything he threw at me, but I couldn't! He was so fast! He was firing off the next move before I could even block the current one. The sound effects made it sound like I was blocking, but I wasn't. How crazy is that? His hands with a weapon were so fast. Untouchable. His back kick is so powerful, too.

RB: When you see that on film, it looks like real contact.

AC: He could really kick you!

RB: On a lot of Hong Kong films, the crew used to turn up, look around, and work out what they could do there and then. On Martial Law, was there any rehearsal or was it more spontaneous?

AC: We had rehearsals. I remember that was the first time we used a mini tv to shoot rehearsals for the choreography, which we edited that same night. That become more common after that.

RB: You've worked under Jackie and Sammo. Do they have different ways of working?

AC: Completely different. Sammo, if he was the director, wouldn't handle the choreography. Whereas Jackie would. He'd choreograph all the time.

RB: When he was the action director, how did Sammo approach the choreography?

AC: He didn't need much rehearsal. He tried to include everything that he could do personally. He'd play to strengths depending on which hand or foot you were better at fighting with. Jackie didn't really do that.

RB: Would Sammo listen to ideas on set?

AC: Yeah, of course. You had to have a good reason, though! He'd question you, and if it was a bad idea, he'd tell you. He's openminded.

RB: Sammo and Jackie are geniuses. They can do so much, in so many roles. I don't know if Sammo can edit, though?
AC: Of course! They edit in their minds all the time. They are really professional.

RB: Do you believe that their Peking Opera training made them very versatile?

AC: It definitely helped them to do multiple things. People in the business have to learn what they can't do. Sammo and Jackie came into the business multi-talented, able to do everything already.

RB: Did you watch any of Sammo's films while you were growing up?

AC: Yes. He starred in many, many good movies. Enter the Fat Dragon, Prodigal Son, and his ghost films. My first movie as a stuntman was with Sammo Hung – Pantyhose Hero.

RB: I was really impressed with Sammo's acting in the 2016 film, My Beloved Bodyguard.

AC: I liked it. A good movie. He's a good actor.

RB: He's great in Heart of the Dragon with Jackie.

AC: That is one of my favourite movies! Every time I watch it, I cry. I like big stunts in films, but I like good stories too. I like Drunken Master 2 as well.

RB: Finally, would you like to work with Sammo again?

AC: Yes! I'd love to. I'd love to work with any of the legends. We almost got him involved in Shang Chi. We offered him Yuen Wah's character, but we couldn't arrange a deal.

RB: I didn't know that! Well, thank you very much for talking to us, Andy, and offering your insights.

AC: My pleasure.

5 FINGERS OF DISCS

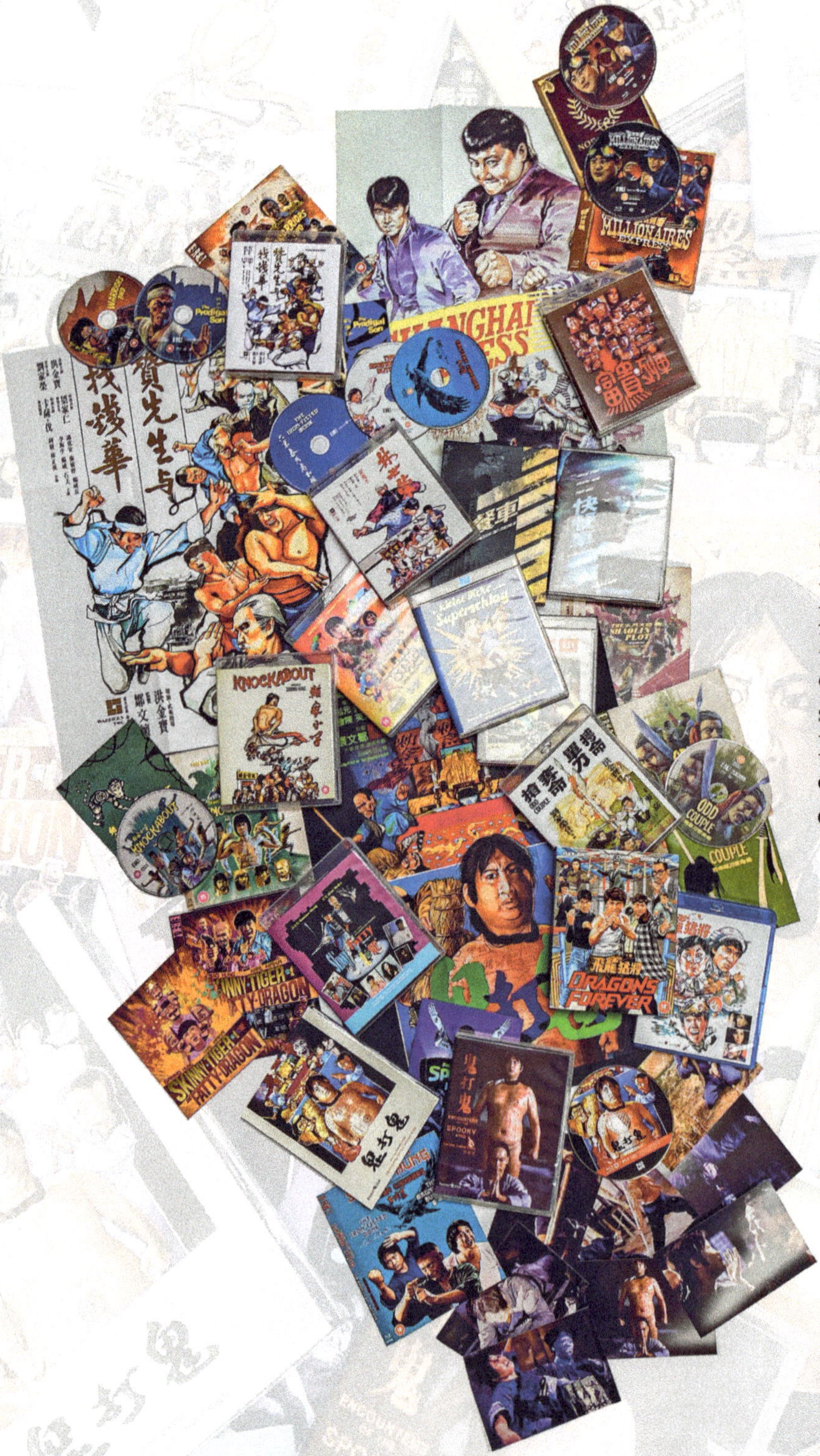

Greetings dear friends, Dragon here once more to weigh in on the heaviest heavy weight that ever did heavy in HK (say that three times with your mouth full of cake). The one, the only, the incomparable Sammo Hung Kam-bo, star of this special issue. The formidable Director/Star/Choreographer and Producer is currently enjoying somewhat of a long overdue Renaissance, or a 'Sammoissance' if you prefer thanks almost exclusively to Eureka Entertainment, who over the past year or two have been putting out a fantastic selection of the Big man's greatest hits. Let's take a look at a few of the titles most deserving of your attention and your hard earned cash.

**1) Three Films by Sammo Hung
The Iron Fisted Monk (1977) / The Magnificent Butcher (1979) / Eastern Condors (1987)
Dir - Sammo Hung
Eureka Entertainment - Region B**

If you only pickup one single release from the many titles listed in this article, make it this one, three absolute gems from Sammo Hung's extensive back catalogue showcasing not just his incredible work as an actor but also his progression as a director. The set kicks off with Sammo's directorial debut, the fantastic (and still very hard hitting) Iron Fisted Monk from 1977 with Sammo starting to assemble the insanely talented team of actors and stuntmen around him that he would go on to use in countless other movies whilst also finding his feet as a director with his now trademark brutality present in the action sequences and the odd mix of dark comedy and tragedy sitting sometimes uncomfortably close to each other. He is backed up by the wonderful Chen Hsing playing the titular Iron Fisted Monk along with my all time favourite Kung Fu baddie, the amazing Fung Hark-On here playing a truly despicable Manchu official with a predilection for Rape that often puts many fans off this movie, but stick with it, there is much here to celebrate in terms of Sammo's action staging and camera work. And the excellent remastered Eureka release gives us Cantonese and English audio options for the movie along with an excellent commentary track from The master of Remaster himself, the wonderful Frank Djeng.

The second film on the set is the absolute classic The Magnificent Butcher, directed by Yuen Woo Ping with Sammo here playing Butcher Lam aka Lam Sai Wing the famed pupil of the legendary Wong Fei Hung (played here by the wonderful Kwan Tak Hing). The film was designed as a somewhat sequel to Drunken Master and had originally cast Simon Yuen aka Yuen Siu Tin (Woo Ping's father who had played the role of Beggar So in Ping's Drunken Master) though sadly Siu Tin died early in production from a Heart Attack and his role was recast by Fan Mei-sheng (the father of Louis Fan of Story of Ricky fame) and despite the problems during production this no doubt caused, The Magnificent Butcher remains one of my favourite Yuen Woo Ping movies.

The choreography is first rate and Hung's performance of Butcher Lam is a role extremely well suited to him. Villain duties are handled principally by the incomparable Lee Hoi-San ably assisted (of course) by Fung Hark-On.

The movie again gives us Cantonese and English audio dubs and a commentary track by Action Movie commentary regulars Big Mike Leeder and Arne Venema.

The third film on the set is the movie that inspired Ricky to name Eastern Heroes, Eastern Eeroes! The phenomenal war movie, Eastern Condors (1987).
Arguably Sammo's greatest film as director (I maybe slightly prefer Millionaires Express) and easily the most enjoyable war movie to come out of HK.
With Sammo assembling an all star cast that would include his future wife Joyce Godeki alongside several of his former Peking Opera School classmates, Yuen Biao, Yuen Wah, Cory Yuen and his frequent collaborator Lam Ching-ying.
The story revolves around Sammo's 'Dirty Dozen' being sent behind enemy lines into Vietnam to destroy a top secret munitions base and coming face to face and toe to toe with Yuen Wah's facial tick laden villain (offering a glimpse of what would follow with his villain turn in Dragon's Forever). The action flows thick and fast and is more bombastic and explosive than usual. Some massive explosions here including one which very nearly cost Chin Kar-lok his life, he was burned extensively in one of the film's many fire stunts. Sammo got into incredible shape for the film, losing over 30lbs and slimming down to a leaner, meaner size than can be seen in his more comedic roles.
Two cuts of the film are on offer here, the full uncut version of the movie alongside the shorter international edit. Commentary duties are once again handled by Mike Leeder and Arne Venema and there is a great TV feature taken from the 1987 miss Hong Kong Pagent with Hung, Yuen Biao and Yuen Wah all performing on stage that's an absolute delight to see.
The only criticism of the set overall is that eastern Condors is more than deserving of a standalone special edition of its own, but it's just great to have the movie looking and sounding so good and the fact you get two other classic movies alongside it, makes this

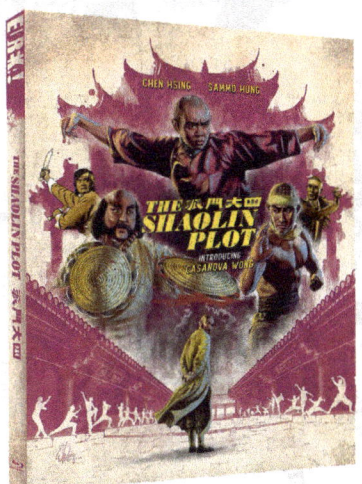

set an absolute no-brainer.
Buy it now!

**2) The Shaolin Plot (1976)
Dir - Huang Feng
Eureka Entertainment
Region B**

Directed by Huang Feng who would later go on to co-write Sammo's debut feature the Iron Fisted Monk and starring many of the same actors who would go on to work on that movie, The Shaolin Plot has been long overlooked by many fans and thankfully this recent release from Eureka should see that changing. It's an incredible movie. Jam packed with some truly stunning choreography (all action designed by Sammo hung) and with Sammo playing a villain's role here (with a great half bald haircut, moustache-beard combo and some excellent flying guillotine-esque weapons). The titular plot revolves around Chen Hsing's efforts to secure all the kung fu manuals from the main schools to use for his own nefarious plans, the last holdouts are those pesky monks at the Shaolin temple and so he goes undercover as a Mute and Deaf Monk to attempt to steal the books from under the monks noses. Ot's up to our hero, James Then to thwart his scheme. Almost wall to wall action ensues. Some stunning temple locations courtesy of the film's Korean locations and a co-starring role from the insanely talented leg fighter, Korean actor Cassanova Wong (to whom Sammo would later give a starring role in Warriors Two). This film is insanely good fun. Highly recommended.

Two excellent commentary tracks on this one, both are a great mix of informative and entertaining in equal measure. One track by Eureka regulars Big Mike Leeder and Arne Venema and a second solo track by the always fantastic Frank Djeng.

Cover art for the release is provided by Darren Wheeling, if you get in early enough you'll get a slipcase and booklet with notes by James Oliver.

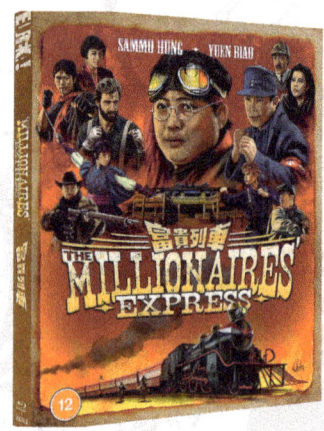

3) Millionaires Express (1978)
Dir - Sammo Hung
Eureka Entertainment
Region B

For me, Sammo's best film overall, a Chinese New Year release with a spectacular all star cast who come together to deliver one of the best Action comedies to ever come out of HK. Lots of Western parallels in this one, but with pure, undiluted Hong Kong stunt and action choreography. It's also one of the best Yuen Biao movies given he has arguably a bigger role in the movie than Sammo himself does.

The plot is fairly simple, Sammo's character returns to his hometown to open up a brothel, and finds the town in disrepair. so plans to set off a bomb on the train tracks forcing a trainload of potential customers to disembark at the town. Throw in a group of Japanese Ninjas on the train in possession of a treasure map and a gang of outlaws out to Rob said Ninjas (and anyone else they can find). Constant sparring between corrupt firefighters and slightly more righteous cops in the town and then throw all these elements together with as much slapstick comedy and action sequences as you can cram in and you get damn good time.

Eureka's release of the movie contains multiple versions of the film including a new Hybrid cut which includes lots of previously deleted scenes and various edits from different cuts of the movie and combines them all into a new, longer 'ultimate cut'.

A brand new Interview with Cynthia Rothrock, as well as Archival interviews (from the old Hong Kong Legends DVD) with Rothrock, Richard Norton, Yuen Biao, Yukari Oshima and the big man himself, Sammo Hung.

We also get two excellent commentary tracks, one from Mike Leeder and Arne Venema as well as another standalone Frank Djeng track.

Cover art for the release is provided by Darren Wheeling (who has created almost all of the Sammo Hung releases covers for Eureka).

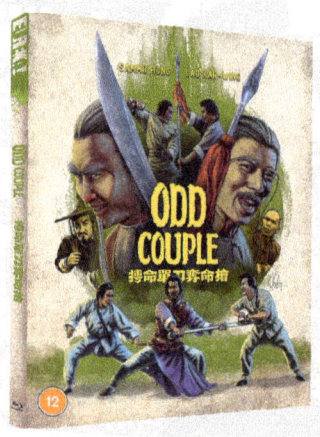

4) The Odd Couple (1982)
Dir - Lau Kar Wing
Eureka Entertainment
Region B

One of the two best Martial Arts Weapons movies ever made (Lau Kar Leung's Legendary Weapons of China being the other). This is easily the best comedy directed by Lau Kar Wing (brother of Lau Kar Leung) who also acts here alongside Sammo Hung in this fantastic Kung Fu comedy, both men playing two different roles in the film, each play one young and one old part, with the younger man becoming the other's older man's student (that confused the hell out of me just typing it, makes sense when you see the film). Two ageing Kung Fu masters meet every ten years to try and find out who is the better fighter, always coming up in a draw, so they opt to each take on a pupil, train the pupil up and then have them fight and whoever wins that match will be the winner. The plot allows for some truly jaw dropping Sword Vs Spear battles, some of the finest ever captured on film. Lau Kar Wing often gets slightly overshadowed by his Big Brother, but this movie proves his acting and directing abilities were every bit as sophisticated. A fantastic film, lovingly restored.

The Eureka version looks absolutely incredible, ports over archival interviews with Lau Kar Wing and co-star Leung Kar-yan as well as two commentaries from, you guessed it.

Big Mike Leeder and Arne Venema on one track, Frank Djeng on the other.

Art is once again provided by Darren Wheeling (with a reversible cover also featuring the original HK poster art).

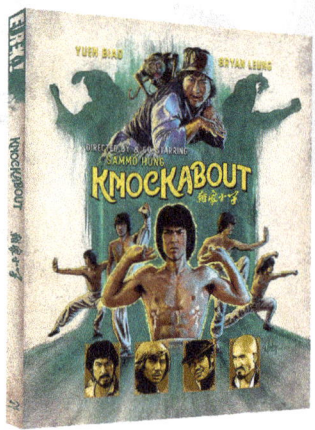

5) Knockabout
Dir - Sammo Hung
88 Films
Region B

Another recent release from Eureka, and coming at the tip of a whole bunch of remastered Yuen Biao titles this year, this is one of Biao's first starring roles, Directed by Sammo Hung and giving Biao a chance to play alongside the wonderful Leung Kar-yan and Lau Kar Wing in this tale of two brothers first conned, then trained and finally bested by a ruthless Kung Fu Killer who have to learn Kung Fu from a mysterious beggar to take revenge. This was always one of the rarest and most expensive Hong Kong Legends DVD's to track down and this new Blu-Ray release effectively ports over all the best extras from that disc (archival interviews with Leung Kar-yan, Sammo Hung and Monkey Kung Fu Master Chan Sau Chang).

And adds two new commentary tracks (Mike

Leeder/Arne Venema and Frank Djeng) as well as a booklet with notes from James Oliver and all new cover art once again from Darren Wheeling.

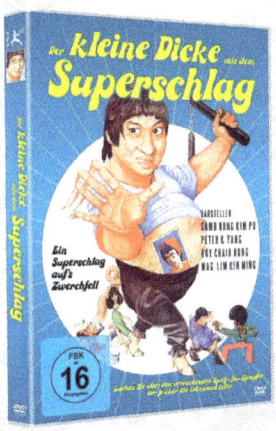

6) Skinny Tiger, Fatty Dragon (1990)
Dir - Sammo Hung
Eureka Entertainment
Region B

Another Lau Kar Wing directed title, this time a contemporary buddy buddy cop story pairing a Bruce Lee obsessed Sammo Hung alongside Karl Maka (star of the Aces go Places movies, who also has a small cameo role in The Odd Couple), with the two cops going toe to toe against a group of ruthless triads led by the director himself, Lau Kar Wing. As much a comedy as it is an action film, but very well staged with some truly excellent action sequences peppered throughout the movie. Notable also for featuring the wonderful Ni Kuang in a rare acting role, here playing Sammo's dad and including his own actual voice (not dubbed by another actor, which at this point in Hk cinema was immensely rare).

This is still available as a two disc set including a wonderful documentary focused on Mark Haughton (I am The White Tiger) student of the legendary Lau Kar Leung and regular HK stuntman, martial artist and action director throughout the 80's and 90's. Extras on the movie itself include two new commentaries, the now standard Mike and Arne track as well as Frank Djeng, this time Frank is joined by martial artist/actor Robert "Bobby" Samuels for his track, Samuels makes a wonderful co-host with Frank and the two play well off of each other.

Cover art is again provided by Darren Wheeling, slipcase and booklet also there if you get in early enough (limited to 3000 copies).

7) Enter The Fat Dragon aka 'Der kleine Dicke mit dem Superschlag' (1978)
Dir - Sammo Hung
Thunderfist Productions
German Import

Stepping away from Eureka this time and jumping over to Germany, to the small label Thunderfist productions, who have recently re-released their 2018 Blu-ray edition of Sammo's fantastic Enter the Fat Dragon as a standard release (it was previously available in media book format). Sammo's second movie as Director after the Iron Fisted Monk and showcasing his very best Bruce Lee impression (he doesn't bust it out that often, only really here, in the aforementioned Skinny Tiger, Fatty Dragon and briefly in his fight with Cynthia Rothrock at the end of Millionaires Express).

The film is one half parody of Bruce Lee's Way of The dragon and one half a parody of bruceploitation movies in general. Sammo plays Ah Long, a pig farmer obsessed with Bruce Lee who moves to the big city to earn a living working at his uncle's restaurant and there finds gangsters causing trouble and is forced to intervene. The Thunderfist release features three different cuts of the movie:
The restored international export cut (93 mins), a reconstructed HK theatrical version (96mins) and the German Theatrical Version (82 mins).
We get English, German and Cantonese Audio as well as a commentary track originally recorded for the Podcast on Fire podcast by Stewart Sutherland, Kenneth Brorsson and Mike Leeder.
You can pickup the disc via Amazon.de

8) Dragons Forever (1988)
Dir - Sammo Hung / Jackie Chan
88 Films
Original Special Edition - Region B
4K Special Edition - Releasing - 22.08.22 UK / 23.08.22 US
US Standard Edition - Region A - Releasing - 23rd Aug 2022

The last outing together onscreen for Jackie Chan, Sammo Hung and Yuen Biao Dragon's Forever remains one of the standout examples of classic Hong Kong Action cinema, albeit one that underperformed at the box office, maybe largely down to all three actors wanting to play against type, Jackie Plays a Lawyer, Yuen Biao a mentally handicapped conspiracy theorist and Sammo hung an arms dealer!
But the action on display here, and the frequent Marx Brothers-esque slapstick battles between our three leads are a joy to

behold.
The plot revolves around Jackie's lawyer initially hired to defend a shady businessman/Drug Kingpin (played with relish and zeal by Yuen Wah) and his attempts to get a local fishery owner to back down from her law suit against his client, who mid film realises he's backing the wrong horse and swaps sides to fight against Yuen Wah's villain. An incredible final reel battle between Chan and Benny The Jet Urquidez

remains one of JC's best hand to hand battles on screen,
Jackie is rarely as intense in combat as when being directed by Sammo Hung.
It's a film I suspect almost everyone reading this already has in their collection.
88 films have released this movie twice in the UK, once in a 2 Disc Special Edition showcasing stunning cover art by Kung Fu Bob O'Brien and also as one of their two steelbook releases
(the steelbook featuring cover art by Thomas Newman).
But with 88's recent foray into releasing titles Stateside, this is getting a fresh coat of cover art paint, thanks to new kid on the block Sean Longmore and a 4K upgrade here in the UK (it's also being released as a standard Blu-Ray in the US, with Longmore's artwork, both will be deluxe editions). An all new commentary track is being provided for the new release by Frank Djeng

9) Wheels On Meals (1984)
Dir - Sammo Hung
Eureka Entertainment
Region B

The other great Yuen Biao/Sammo Hung and Jackie Chan feature (Project A always felt more like a Jackie Chan movie with cameos from the other two).
Wheels on Meals moves the action away from HK to Barcelona and take full advantage of the location showcasing some fo the city's most iconic architecture.

Jackie and Yuen Biao's food truck operating heroes finding themselves pulled into a kidnapping plot against Lola Forner by their Private detective friend Sammo.
Another incredible Jackie Vs Beenie The Jet finale in this. one of the all time classics and another that is likely already on everyone's shelves by this point, but just in case not, the Eureka version has most of the old Hong Kong Legends extras ported over.
If you have the Eureka edition already or if you crave something a little bit different, there is also a great HK edition with a Full slipcover from Fortune Star and a tasty Novamedia edition from Korea, but neither has as good extras as on the Eureka version.

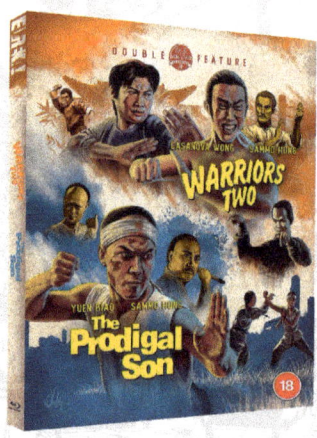

10) Warriors Two (1978) / The Prodigal Son (1981)
Dir - Sammo Hung
Eureka Entertainment

A double feature from Eureka, this time pairing Sammo's two incredible Wing Chun focused movies, Warriors Two and the Prodigal Son. Both absolute standouts in his filmography. warriors Two sees Cassanova Wong taking centre stage in a rare leading role alongside Sammo, both students of Leung Kar Yan's master Jan facing of against a ruthless gang of business men who have a stranglehold on the town.
Led by the wonderful Fung Hark-On here getting to show off his considerable Mantis Fist talents as the villainous Banker Mo.
Two cuts of the movie are on the set, the HK Theatrical cut (95 mins) and the shorter International export cut (90mins).
A making of Warriors two featurette and two commentary tracks,
Frank Djeng again joined by Robert Samuels and the good old boys, Mike Leeder and Arne Venema with their usual and very welcome mix of chuckles and facts.

The Prodigal Son again showcases the wonderful skills of Yuen Biao, playing a delusional rich kid whose father has paid off everyone in the town to lose to him giving him a false sense that he's a Kung Fu expert who finally falls foul of some visiting Opera performers who give him a solid ass kicking, after being humiliated by the Opera performer Leung Yee-tai (played by the incredible Lam Ching Ming) after the troupe fall foul of the Martial Arts expert son of a Machu Duke, played by Frankie Chan who attempted to assassinate the troupe. Yuen Biao helps Leung Yee Tai to escape and is finally taken in by Leung Yee-tai and his friend Wong Wah-bo (played by Sammo Hung) who train him and he returns to face off against Frankie Chan in an explosive all out battle of Wing Chun magic!
The Prodigal Son discs offers up archival interview with Sammo Hung, Yuen Biao, Frankie Chan and Guy Lai and two more commentary tracks, again by Frank Djeng / Robert Samuels and Mike Leeder / Arne Venema. A truly stunning set of two classic slices of Kung Fu genius.
Cover art is once more provided by Eureka regular Darren Wheeling.

11) Winners and Sinners (1983) / My Lucky Stars (1985) /
Twinkle Twinkle Lucky Stars (1985)
Dir - Sammo Hung
Eureka Entertainment
Region B

The other great triple bill put out by Eureka, brings together the three best of the Lucky Stars movies, the three directed by and starring Sammo Hung with every increasing in scale cameos by Jackie Chan and Yuen Biao (and a young Andy Lau by the time we get to Twinkle Twinkle).
These are largely ensemble comedy movies

with Sammo being joined by Richard Ng and Stanley Fung in all three movies showcasing lots of slapstick comedy which slightly overshadows more traditional kung fu movie sequences, but as the films progress the action intensifies adding female bodybuilder and martial artist Michiko Nishiwaki and Dick Wei in for My Lucky Stars and Richard Norton and Yuasaki Kurata stepping into the mix as villains in the third movie.

All three are great fun, but the second two parts are far more rewatch able than the first.

My Lucky Stars moves the action to Japan and Twinkle Twinkle takes the gang to Thailand
(and back again to HK)
Commentaries on all three movies are provided by Frank Djeng and most of the old special features from the Hong Kong Legends DVD's have also been ported over, including a great interview with Michiko Nishiwaki from My Lucky Stars and with Richard Norton on Twinkle Twinkle Lucky Stars.

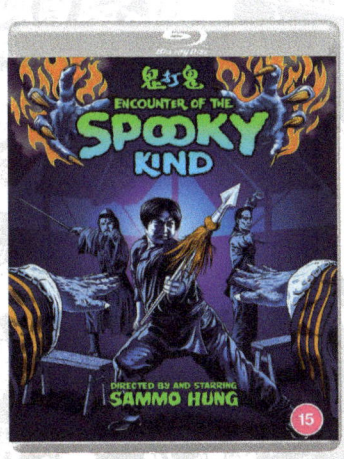

12) Encounter of the Spooky Kind (1980)
Dir - Sammo Hung
Eureka Entertainment
Region B

Bringing together kung fu, special effects and blending in heaps of Chinese horror stories and folklore, Sammo created the wonderful Encounters of the Spooky Kind in 1980. Starring in the main role Sammo plays Courageous Cheung, a man seemingly known for his lack of fear, who comes face to face with ever increasingly intense spirits and eventually hoping vampires after his cheating wife's new partner decides to hire a taoist priest to curse him. The story is actually pretty convoluted to explain here, but the action sequences are immensely inventive and extremely well staged, the effects hold up for the most part (practical mostly) and the film is a Halloween staple in my household alongside the Sammo Hung produced Mr Vampire (also available from Eureka).

This Eureka edition of the movie again gives us a Frank Djeng Commentary track and archival interview with Sammo, even if you don't like Horror movies, this is still highly recommended, it's a great fun film. Artwork is again provided by Darren Wheeling, though there is also a gorgeous Novamedia edition of the movie with the original HK poster as its cover, but lacking Frank Djeng's excellent commentary track.

So that's about all the space I can squeeze out of Ricky for this bumper Sammo Special,
It would take a whole magazine in itself to cover all the various DVD's and Blu-Rays available and to deep dive into the other editions of the movies featured available in other regions, so I've tried here to mostly just cover the main titles still largely accessible in the UK (and in the US if you have a multi region machine. US friends head to OrbitDVD or DiabolikDVD both of whom import the UK Eureka titles)

As i've been assembling this article we are seeing more and more instances of Arrow Video US picking up and re-releasing Eureka titles in the States with the same special features (just with different cover art. The upcoming Angela Mao Double Feature (both also starring Sammo Hung) will come out this way, via Eureka here in the UK and from Arrow Video US in the States.
If these titles continue to sell well hopefully we'll see more and more instances of them being more widely available on both sides of the Atlantic.

Thanks for reading!

See you all next issue or online on the Youtubes, Same Kung Fu-Time, same Kung Fu-channel!

Written by Johnny 'The Fanatical Dragon' Burnett

www.youtube.com/thefanaticaldragon

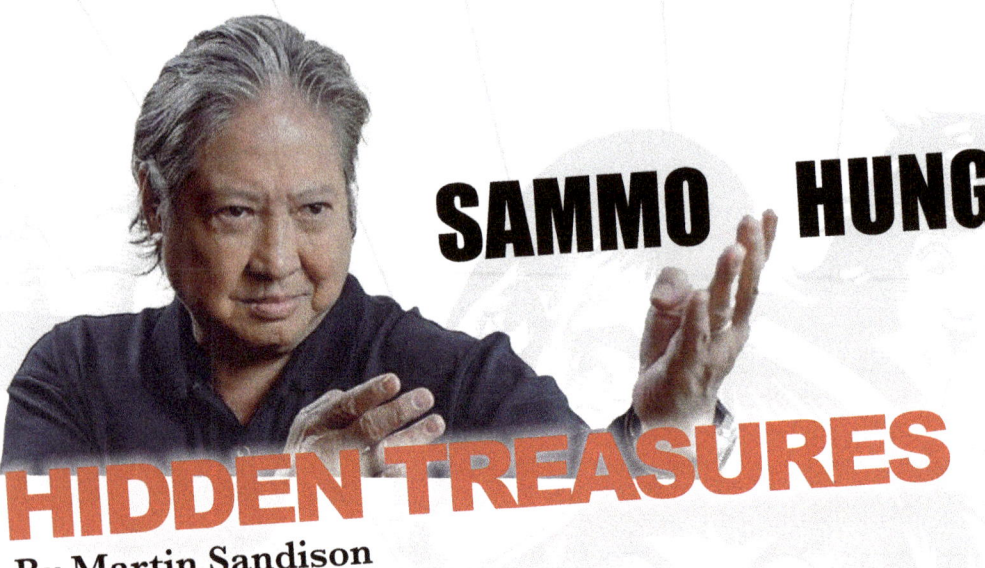

SAMMO HUNG'S HIDDEN TREASURES

By Martin Sandison

From battling Bruce Lee in the opening scene of Enter the Dragon, to Donnie Yen in the final blistering reel of SPL (Killzone), Sammo Hung has seen and done it all when it comes to Hong Kong martial arts movies. He is my ultimate, personal hero, and some years ago I was lucky enough to interview him. Let me tell you, he is as warm, genuine and magnetic in person as in his countless screen classics.

During the 80's and 90's Hung was making so many films that some have not been as recognised as maybe they should. I'd like to take this opportunity to redress that balance, by shedding light on some little-known movies.

A year after his game-changing masterpiece Prodigal Son, Sammo took the directorial reins of the action comedy Carry on Pickpocket. Very much a precursor of the style we all know and love in the form of the Lucky Stars films, with a dash of John Woo's early comedies and action beats that are ahead of its time, the film is a little gem. The comedy ranges from the opening scenes ingenious ways to pick a pocket, to Hong Kong comedic legend Richard Ng's many jokes. You can always rely on him, especially if he's wearing sandals and socks.

The movie is notable as being the first time Dick Wei appeared as the main villain in a Hung production. The two go toe to toe in a fight that is at turns intricate, violent and as Hung does so well, full of impact. You can really see the development of the style which started with Prodigal Son, with a reliance on kickboxing and razor sharp editing. Carry On Pickpocket has a reasonable narrative with Hung's character getting involved with undercover policewoman Deannie Yip, and Hung's humble onscreen persona is given an early outing. This is offset by Frankie Chan's arrogance, and the three make a watchable trio.

In '86 Sammo not only created the all-time classic Millionaire's Express and starred in the fourth Lucky Stars film, he also appeared in the action comedy Where's Officer Tuba?

For many years I wondered why at the start of my VHS of Police Assassins 2 (Yes, Madam), Cynthia Rothrock's introduction to audiences, the opening scene seemed disconnected to the rest of the movie. That scene was in fact the opening of Where's Officer Tuba?, as the real opening of Police Assassins 2 features Yeoh trapping a flasher's penis in an open book. The BBFC, as it was at the time, may have found the scene too racy.

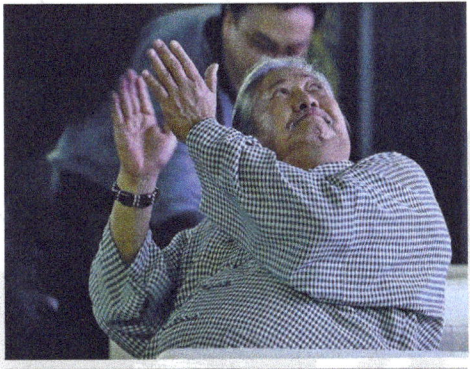

abilities, despite knocking him down! Jackie Cheung battles Chang Yi in a high energy fight that shows the aptitude of Sammo and his team for using doubles; the cutting is so good you can't tell it's not Cheung doing those moves.

Speaking of other cast members there are some real high profile names in the movie, such as Joey Wong who plays Sammo's love interest, David Chiang who is the ghost of the cop who haunts Sammo (Hwang and Chiang have a short fight), and Lam Ching Ying and Corey Yuen Kwai have an amusing cameo as two Taoist priests. Being a Hong Kong film of its type and the time it was made, the plot seems to be made up as it goes along, and some scenes are there just for laughs. In comparison to many of his other films at the time, the laughs don't all hit the mark, and you can tell this is a lesser film in terms of production values. Don't let that put you off! As we all know, Hong Kong movies work wonders with low budgets.

In 1988 Hung co-starred in the movie Paper Marriage with Maggie Cheung, one of the greatest actresses Hong Kong has ever produced. Later in her career she would make films such as In the Mood For Love, which got her known internationally. In the 80's aswell as appearing as Jackie Chan's long-suffering girlfriend in Police Story 1 and 2, she also acted in many other movies, Paper Marriage being a good example of her early style. It's a romantic comedy drama with pepperings of superb action, and takes the lead from the Gerard Depardieu picture Green Card.

Cheung plays Judy Lee, a Hong Konger who wants to move to the States to be with her fiance, but needs a surrogate husband in the interim until she can get residency. Hung is that surrogate, and the two begin a rocky relationship that involves some silly 80's style HK humour, decent drama and the thrills and spills that lead to the obligatory final act with criminal villains led by the ever present Dick Wei. Hung's character arc is actually dealt with well, as at first he's a bit of a misogynist due to bad treatment by his ex-wife (played by Joyce Godenzi, Hung's real-life bride!) but later grows to care for Judy. Paper Marriage is directed by Alfred Cheung, who is perhaps best known for directing the fantastic thriller On the Run, with Hung's Peking Opera brother Yuen Baio.

There are two ring bouts in the film, with Hung taking on one of my favourite film-makers Phillip Ko Fei and that other great Hong Kong villainous actor Billy Chow. Both are fast, brutal and sharply edited, and it's cool to see Hung in this fighting context, something he didn't do too much (the other example I can think of is in Game of Death). The ending is where the real action is at though, as Dick Wei takes on Hung and Billy Chow, and some obligatory gweilos get to show some action chops. Also Chin Kar Lok gets to throw down as a stunt double in his usual incredible martial arts style, throwing

best directors, the late Ringo Lam. There's not a lot of combat, but one night scene shows Hung's mastery of fight direction and Lam's mastery of dark aesthetics. In Painted Faces Sammo plays his real-life Peking Opera Master Yu Jim Yuen, which depicts the lives of the seven little fortunes in the school. In my book and many others this is Hung's best dramatic performance, and the film is a real tear-jerker.

The 80's and 90's were a time in which Sammo Hung came into his own as a martial arts film-maker, and the pictures mentioned are my favourites of his lesser-known output. I'm sure there are those among you who have other picks. Due to a knee operation in 2017, Hung was wheelchair-bound for a couple of years, taking a break from production. Now he's back acting in a couple of productions, so let's hope they are enjoyable and we get to see a different side of a true legend.

a somersault slow motion kick that's one for the ages. Overall it's a fun ride that while not being up there with Sammo's best, is without doubt worth watching.

Come the early 90's Hung continued to work at a breakneck pace. 1990's Pantyhose Hero is a fan favourite, although now the comedy seems very dated and offensive, but boy does the end action sequence deliver in this semi-remake of Al Pacino's 70s classic Cruising. Hung stars alongside singer Alan Tam as two undercover cops who infiltrate Hong Kong's gay scene to find a criminal. Cue many now-cringeworthy homophobic jokes. That's Hong Kong movies of the time, you can either take offence or appreciate that it was a long time ago. The visceral thrills of the end battle Hung delivers with aplomb.

Slickers vs Killers teamed Hung with his offscreen wife Joyce Godenzi in a strange but charming tale with snippets of superb action, although the movie overall underwhelms. A film which could have been much better, but is still very much worth watching, Touch and Go paired Hung with one of Hong Kong's

KELLY HU

Interview by Rick Baker

On February 13th, 1968, a girl of Chinese, English, and Hawaiian ancestry was born in Honolulu, Hawaii. Her father, Herbert, was a salesman and her mother, Juanita, worked many odd jobs to help support the family. She has one older brother, Glenn. She is a former Miss Teen USA, and modelled in Japan and Italy for several months before deciding to relocate to L.A. and try her hand at show business. She received her break on TV's Growing Pains (1985) in 1987 and never looked back. Kelly was also the First Asian-American to be featured on the cover of "Maxim" magazine. That issue was the biggest-selling issue in the magazine's history.

As one of the key characters in "martial Law" playing Chen Pei Pei alongside Sammo Hung   I wanted to reach out to Kelly to find out about her career and what it was like working with Sammo Hung.

I reached out to my good friend Andy cheng who kindly passed a message on to her and Kelly kindly responded with a yes!!
I admit I was a little nervous calling cold, but I was greeted with a very warm smile.
The first thing I notice is how attractive Kelly is, a lady now in her early fifties with flashes of grey looking 15 years younger than the date on her birth certificate.
I welcome Kelly and thank her for talking to me and decide to (after some small talk) compose myself and get down to the job in hand

RB: To start with, could you tell us a little bit about your background?

KH: I was born and raised in Hawaii. My parents were divorced, so my Mom raised us on her own, and struggled to make ends meet. She never had less than three jobs. She was always pinching pennies and trying to find ways to save money.

RB: So she had to budget really carefully?

KH: Oh, yeah! She was on a very, very tight budget. We drank powdered milk, and she would only put the heating on for an hour a day. There was only so much water you could use - so a shower would last for five minutes before it went cold. I got my first job in a clothing store when I was 13 so that I could buy my own clothes for school. I was sick of wearing hand me downs! While I was working that job, I got scouted in the mall for modelling. Back then, a lot of girls who were mixed race (half Asian, half Caucasian – we called them 'hapa haole' in Hawaii) were getting scouted and taken to Japan for modelling jobs. They'd make $20,000 in one summer, and come back and put a down payment on a house. This was back in the 1980s, when that amount of money meant something.

RB: That's a lot of money now!

KH: Not in Hawaii, though. I mean, it's so expensive there. Anyway, the agent who scouted me said that if I entered a pageant, they could use that title to promote me in Japan, and make a lot more money. They didn't really have pageants in Japan, and so they were intrigued by titles and things like that. It didn't really matter which pageant I won – I just had to win a local competition

Page 109 Eastern Heroes Sammo Hung Special

KH: Yeah! That's when pageants were in their heyday.

RB: What's it like to have no money, then suddenly so much money?

KH: Life-changing! For my mother and I. We went from pinching pennies to buying a condo. It also afforded me the opportunity to check out an acting career, which was always something I wanted to do, but I never thought I would have the opportunity. I took drama for every semester of high school, and therefore I never learned how to type, or computers, or any other stuff. I was like, 'Drama, drama, drama!' Right after graduation, I got cast in my first role in Hawaii, in a show called Growing Pains. The Seaver family go to Hawaii on vacation and the producers needed to cast a girl who was a local love interest for Mike Seaver. Before the show even aired, I packed up my bags and moved to Los Angeles. I realised that I had an opportunity. It was all destined! I wasn't 'determined to make it'. Things just seemed to fall together for me. I could not have planned it.

RB: I guess you have a lot of gratitude for the way things worked out?

KH: Absolutely. I'm a strong believer in destiny. I moved to LA with one credit to my name, and then lied about the rest of my resume! Which you can't do anymore, because everyone can look everything up on the internet! I lied about being in plays and student films, but I did have that one

and gain a title. I entered the Miss Hawaii Teen USA pageant because I didn't have to do any stupid talent or anything, and I ended up winning it. I was planning to go to Japan in the summer, but as it turned out, when you win the local pageant, you're obligated to compete in the national pageant, representing your state. I didn't think I'd win the national competition. Being an Asian person from Hawaii in the 1980s, it just didn't seem feasible. I went with the attitude that I'd go, try to have a good time, and then go off in the summer to Japan to do my modelling thing. I ended up winning the Miss Teen USA pageant! This gave me over $100,000 in cash and prizes!

RB: Wow!

legitimate credit! I took out a full page advert in Variety the day that episode premiered and I got twenty calls from agents before it even aired.

RB: A lot of the people from the era, such as Maggie Cheung and Michelle Yeoh, have told me that back then in Hong Kong, to get into the movies you had to win a beauty pageant. Miss TVB, or something. I guess it was the same for you. You won a pageant and the doors opened.

KH: It doesn't really work the same way in the United States. Pageants aren't really respected like they are in Asia. A lot of people, including Miss Universe winners, have expected scripts to just fly onto their desks. That doesn't always happen. You still have to prove yourself. You still have to audition. There's too much money at stake for producers to hire someone just because they won a beauty pageant. You still have to prove that you can act.

RB: What martial arts skills did you gain growing up to put you in good stead?

KH: I didn't grow up with any martial arts background. My brother got sent to kung fu. I got sent to ballet. It wasn't until my late 20s that I started karate. I've always been interested in martial arts. I had a roommate who was getting her black belt. She invited me to her ceremony. I remember watching, in tears, thinking, 'I need to do this!' There was such a strong draw. Destiny, right? Days later, I was in a karate class with the same instructor.

RB: You know, lots of female action stars were very easy to choreograph if they had a ballet background.

KH: Exactly. I had a good sense of my body. Although, everything in ballet is turned 'out', whereas in karate it's turned 'in', so the positioning style is different. I found it hard to work out. Also, I felt like karate was a really good introduction to martial arts on screen for women because it's all about power and straight lines, unlike wushu, which is very graceful and ballet-like. A lot of women on screen can kick high and look graceful, but I don't think they look strong when they're doing martial arts. Karate was a better way for my body to look stronger on camera.

RB: How did you get the gig for Martial Law?

KH: I was already in Nash Bridges with Don Johnson. During the hiatus between seasons, Carlton Cuse (the creator) offered me a role in the pilot for Martial Law. They needed someone to play the villain. After we shot it, they tested it with audiences. My character tested so highly that people wanted to see more! It was only meant to be a guest role, because I was under contract with

Nash Bridges, but they moved me from one show to the other. They said I'd get better storylines because my character was superior in Martial Law. It was kind of a gamble, because it was a new series, but I took it. In the materials advertising the first season, I was barely visible…

RB: Even though you'd scored so highly in the pilot, they kept you in the background?

KH: Yes! I ended up having to do both shows for a month, where they finished my character in one series, and introduced my character in another. It was tough, flying back and forth! Eventually they took Tammy Lauren out of the show and made my character more central, then brought in Arsenio Hall.

RB: Was this the first time you met Sammo Hung?

KH: On the show? Yeah. Oh wait, no. I might have met him socially through Jackie before that. I can't remember exactly! It all kind of happened at the same time.

RB: What was it like working with Sammo? He was very well-respected in Hong Kong as a choreographer and director.

KH: I was very interesting. Before Arsenio came on, it was Sammo's show. He had his two sidekicks, Tammy and Louis Mandylor. He was a very simple guy. He didn't have a huge entourage. His wife was on set a lot to do the translating.

RB: Is that Joyce Godenzi?

KH: We knew her as Mina. Sammo struggled with a lot of the dialogue, because his English was not good. I get that. Whenever I have to do any dialogue in Mandarin I'm in a complete panic! I hate it! They were finally smart enough to give him an earpiece so she could feed him his lines just before he'd have to say them. It was a bit distracting; because it was so loud you could actually hear the lines! At first, I didn't know what was going on, because no one had told us about the earpiece! There was just a voice coming from nowhere!

RB: Did you do your own bits and pieces, or did they get a double in?

KH: They did have an amazing double. Michiko…

RB: Oh, Michiko Nishiwaki? I know her.
KH: You know everyone! You should tell me what I should know! Ha ha ha!

RB: I'm like you. I've been very lucky in life to meet people and have opportunities!
KH: Exactly. So, I did a lot of the fighting stuff, but Michiko would do the jumping and cartwheels. She was incredible and fearless.

RB: She was in a couple of Jackie films. She was a bodybuilder.

KH: Yes! She was very muscular and in very good shape. She doubled me in Scorpion King. After I'd done the water slide scene, I climbed out of the pool and walked over. She looked at me and said, 'Oh, you have a booger,' and she picked it out of my nose! I was like, 'Wait a minute - you've just picked a booger out of my nose!' We'd known each other for ten years, and she was like, 'Oh, I'm a mother – it doesn't bother me.' That's how close I was to her. She was amazing!

RB: Did you have any interest in martial arts movies growing up?

KH: I watched them when I was very young – maybe six or seven years old – but I had no idea who I was watching. My Dad used to take us to Chinatown to watch Hong Kong films, because my brother was four years older, he was taking kung fu, he was a huge Bruce Lee fan, and I remember seeing things like Enter the Dragon. I just recall being traumatised. My parents had divorced by this point, and my Dad didn't know what to do with us to entertain us, so he would take us to these films. There was always so much blood and guts!

RB: I'm surprised they let you in!

KH: I know! I don't think they would nowadays. Back then there was no such thing as ratings, and it was Chinatown, so they didn't care who you brought. I remember specifically this one scene where one guy was doing a short punch. He would go through a chopboard and pull his fist back over and over again. In the big fight at the end, he punches through someone's stomach and rips out their guts. That horrified me! They were fun films if you were older and you knew it was all fake.

RB: It can scar you for life!

KH: I'm scarred for life! It took me a little while to appreciate just the martial arts part.

RB: Did you do any socialising with Sammo?

KH: Not really! We were working too hard. Maybe I wasn't well-liked enough (laughs).

RB: Do you have any stories from the set?

KH: It was so long ago! I remember that Louis always told great stories. He always made it so much fun to be on set. Sammo didn't speak English very much, so it was hard to…

RB: That's interesting, because when I met him in the 90s, he spoke great English! This was before Martial Law!

KH: Oh!

RB: Maybe he just felt more relaxed to speak English off-camera.

KH: Also, maybe it's because off-camera, in conversation, he's only using words that he knows, whereas reading an English script full of unfamiliar words is different. He had to memorise verbatim all this dialogue. At first they gave him way too much dialogue, which was really frustrating for him, so they had to cut the amount right down. Maybe that's why they brought in Arsenio? Also, with the success of Rush Hour, they really tried to do that whole Rush Hour thing…

RB: That's maybe why Martial Law happened. When I met Sammo, he never really believed that he would cross over to America. He didn't

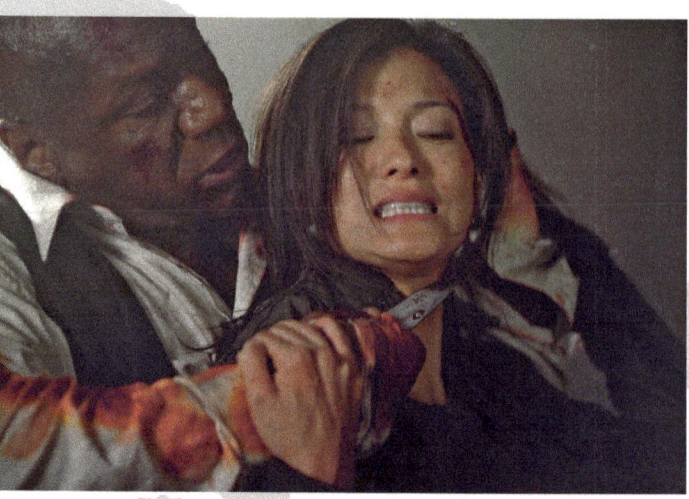

think he had that star appeal like Jackie. Then people like Quentin Tarantino were raving about the action and the stunts in Hong Kong. John Woo went to America. Rush Hour was a success. So maybe it gave Sammo the confidence to try. And he did gain a lot of fans. He came across well in the show. Even at the time, though, I felt like they'd given him too much dialogue, and he should have been shown more as a fish out of water.

KH: Yes, exactly. I think he would have been better served as a silent but deadly character. It worked a bit better that way when Arsenio came on, because he could be the clown. Sammo could do his little sharp barbs at him. Sammo, to his credit, was one of the very first Asian series leads. There's barely been one since. It's time that there was another.

RB: There's been a lot more Asian actors and actresses in the last five years doing well in films. Look at Michelle Yeoh's new film – Everything Everywhere All At Once.

KH: She is amazing. She is the QUEEN of that genre! When I first came to LA in the mid-1980s, there were only a handful of Asian actors. Me, Tia Carrere, Tamlyn Tomita. Vivian Wu was doing a little bit of work. Rosalind Chao, too.

RB: What happened when you finished the season? Did it open up other opportunities in a similar 'action, fighting girl' vein?

KH: That's all anybody ever saw me as! Even when I did Scorpion King, all of the interviews and publicity was people asking me, 'Oh, so you really kick ass in this film?' If you watch it, I literally hold a sword twice! I don't really do anything ass-kicking wise in the film. But after Martial Law, people just assume that every time I do something on-screen, I'm going to kick ass.

RB: And did you get to do any of that in other films?

KH: Yeah, right after Scorpion King I had that great scene with Hugh Jackman in X Men 2. I did a lot of zombie movies, or action films, that I wish nobody saw! I think that after Martial Law, people saw Asian women as regulars on screen.

RB: In Hong Kong movies, women were always empowered. They kicked and punched men, and were right at the forefront of the action.

KH: I always seem to play an assassin, or a cop! In the series I'm doing at the moment, BMF, I play a cop. It's based on a true story about drug dealers.

RB: Did you feel like the second season of Martial Law was quite dark, compared to the first?

KH: To be honest, I don't remember! (laughs)

RB: A few people have suggested that that's why it ended.

KH: I think the reason the series ended was because it got too expensive. There was some behind the scenes stuff going on that I wasn't privy to. Production always seemed to be getting shut down due to some kind of disagreement. You'll have to ask Sammo!

RB: He's not very well at the moment, I don't know if you know. A lot of the stunts and things have caught up with him. He loves his food, too.

KH: And his whiskey and cigars!

RB: Yeah! So he's not in a great place. Can I just say, you're looking fantastic! Any tips?

KH: Thank you! I've actually lost ten pounds recently because I've got some love scenes coming up. At 54 years old, I'm finally going to do nudity! Why this long?! Why couldn't it have come along when I was already skinny and in great shape? Although, I love being in my fifties! I feel like I'm beginning to understand the world.

RB: People take care of themselves so well these days.

KH: They do. I enjoyed taking a break during the pandemic. I was very careful about who I was in contact with, because I have asthma and elderly parents, so I liked just spending time at home. I also started a t-shirt company that promotes simple messages, promoting unity and celebrating diversity. I sell them through my website – 33edge.com.

RB: That's great! I'll not keep you any longer, Kelly. Thank you very much for your time!

KH: No problem, thank you. Have a great day!

SELECTED FILMOGRAPHY

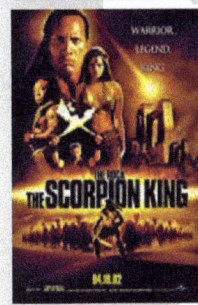
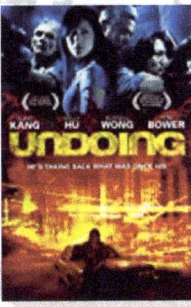

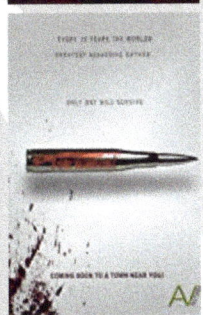
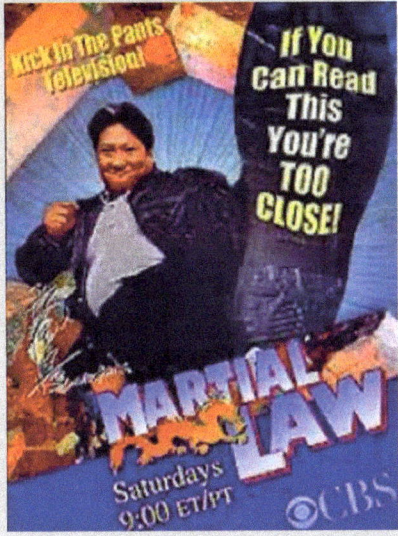

JAPANESE MEMORABILIA
From Mike Nesbitt's collection

BROCHURES

LADY KUNG FU
アンジェラ·マオの女活殺拳
LADY
KUNG FU
定価 150円

スカイ·ハイ
TOWA
東宝
スカイ·ハイ
日比谷映画劇場

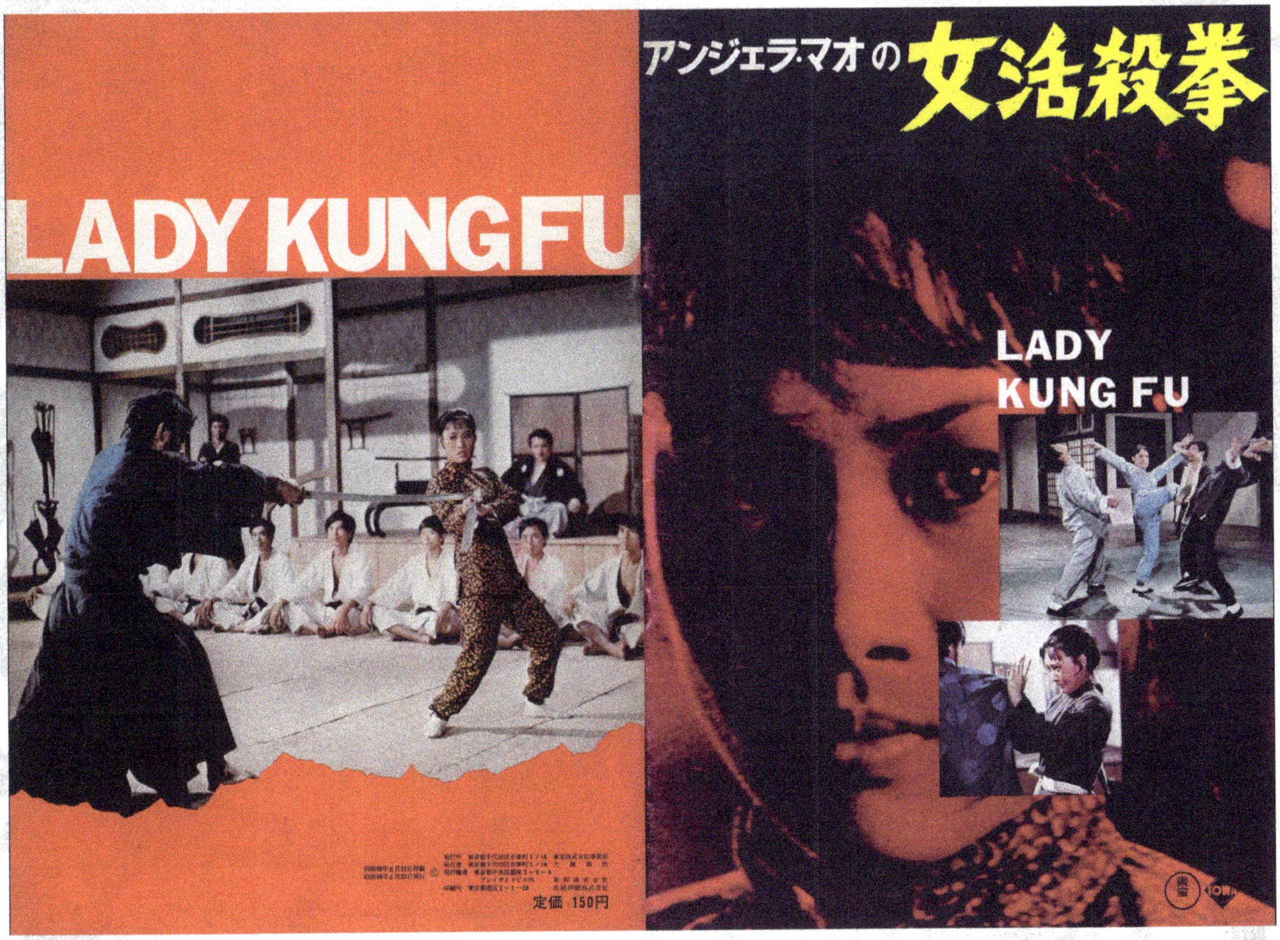

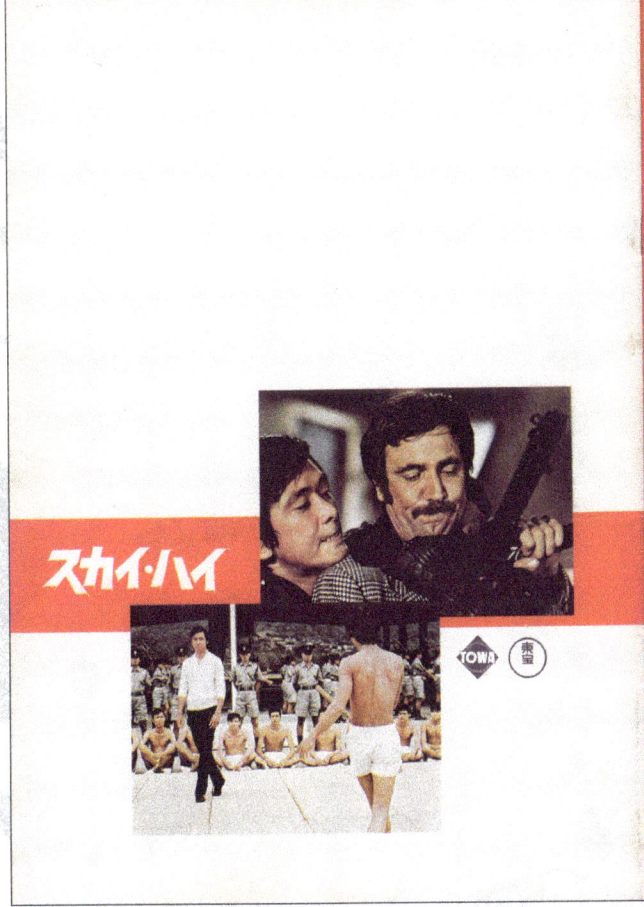

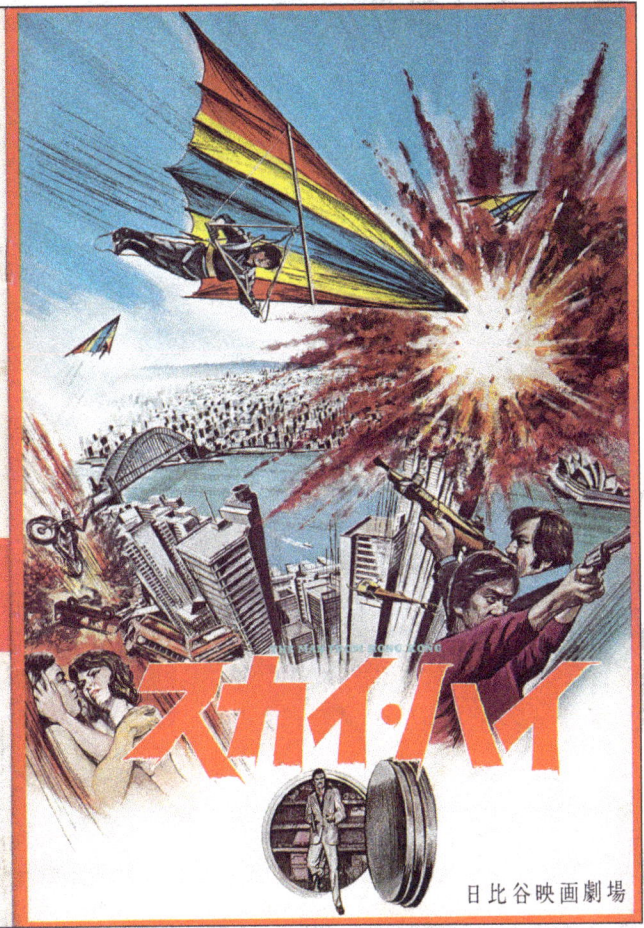

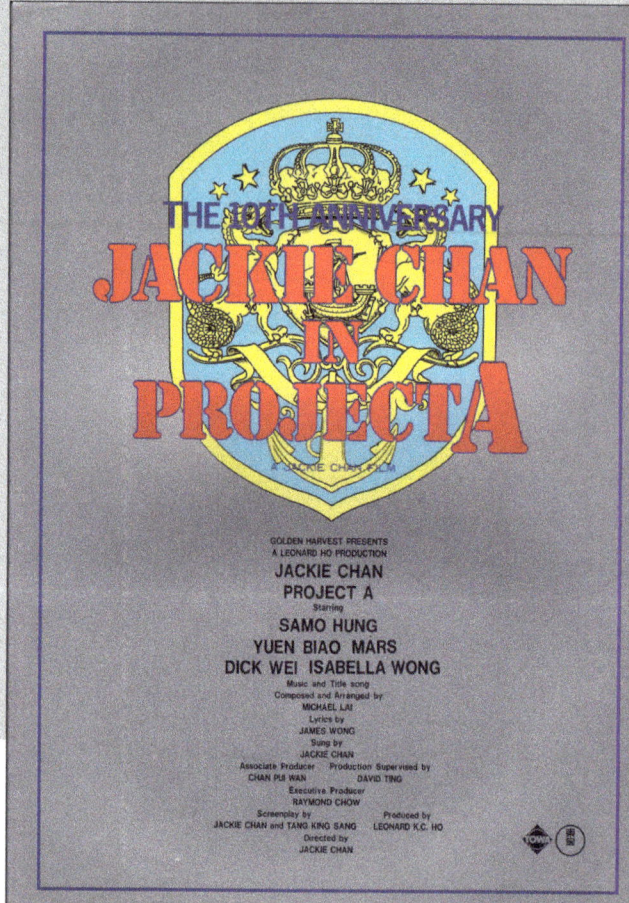

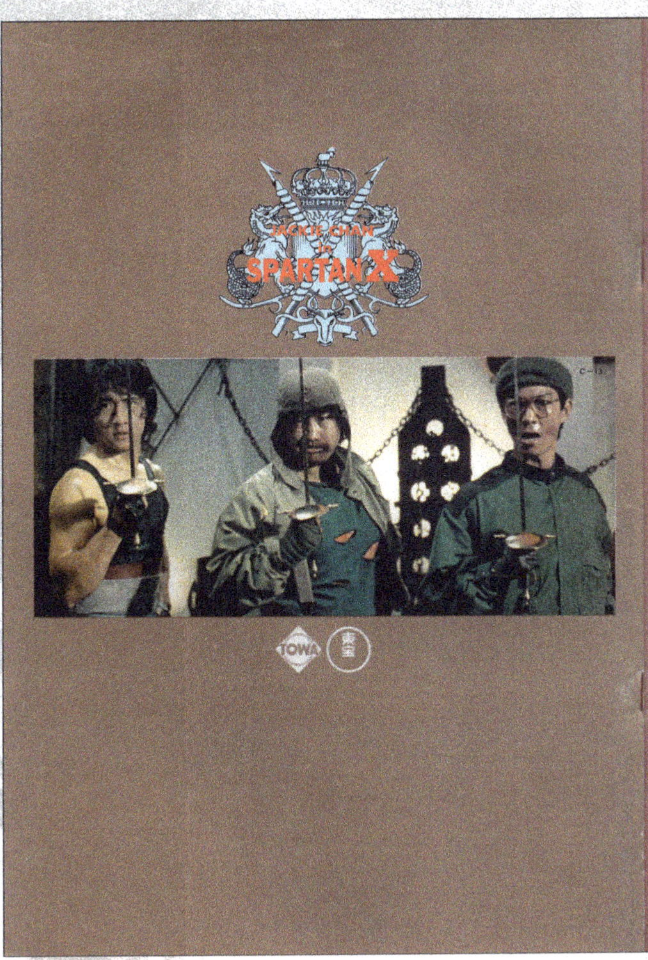

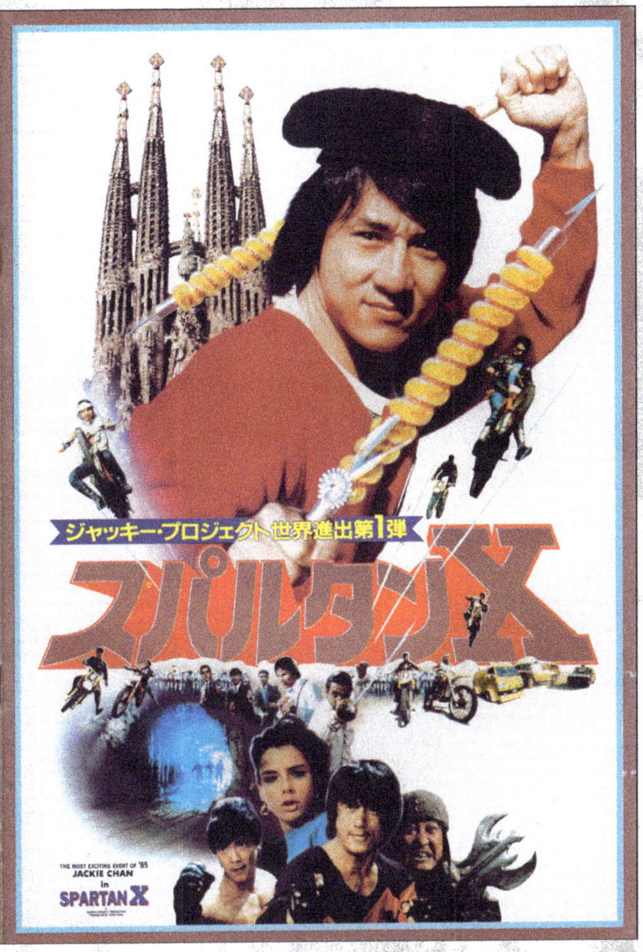

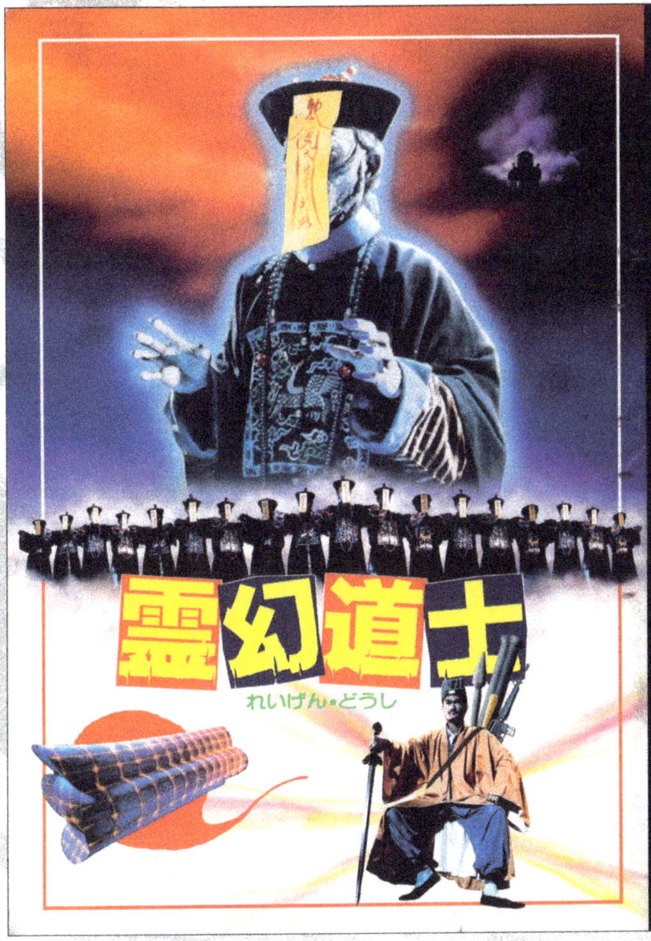

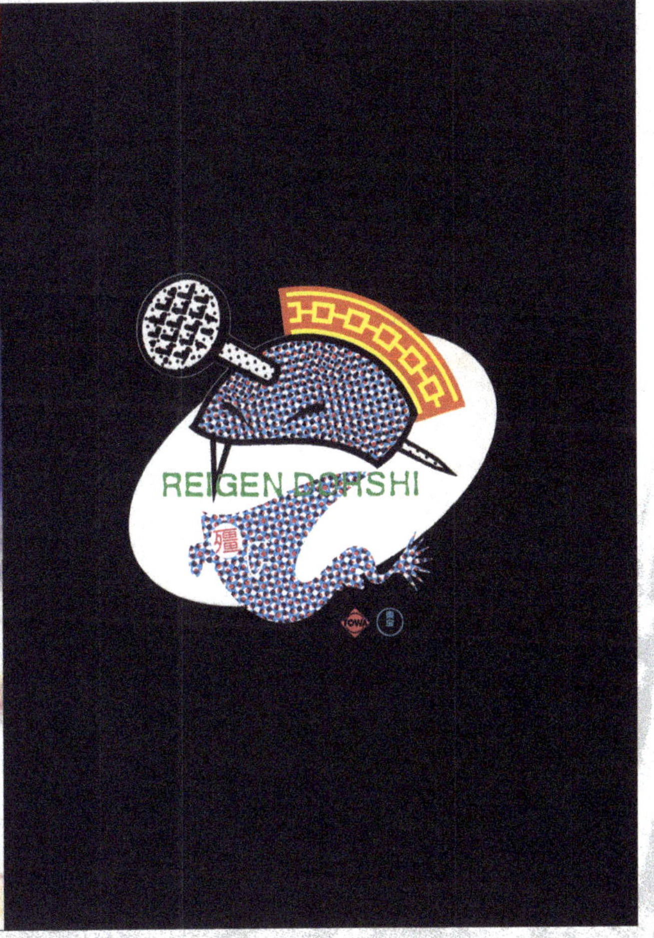

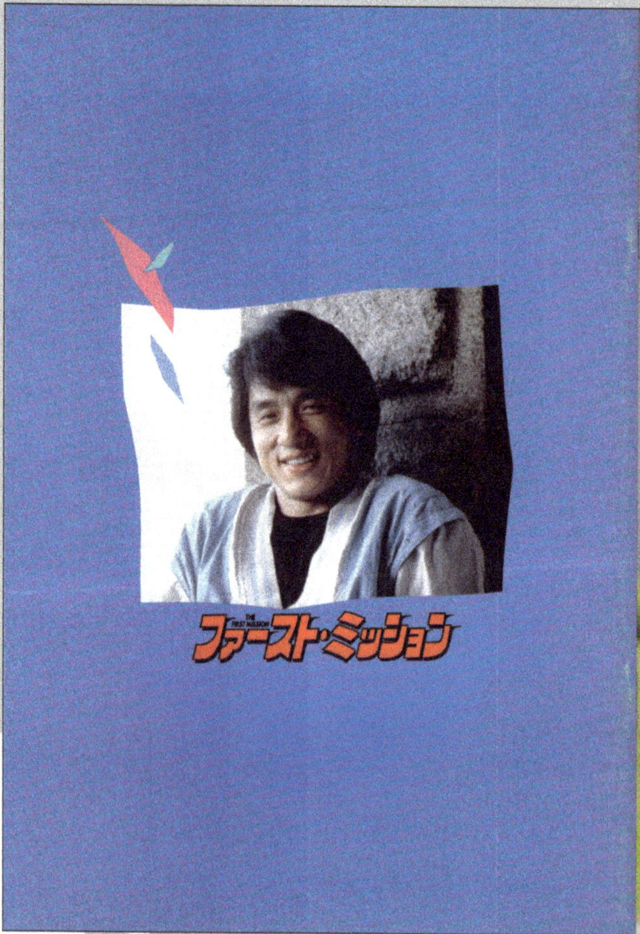

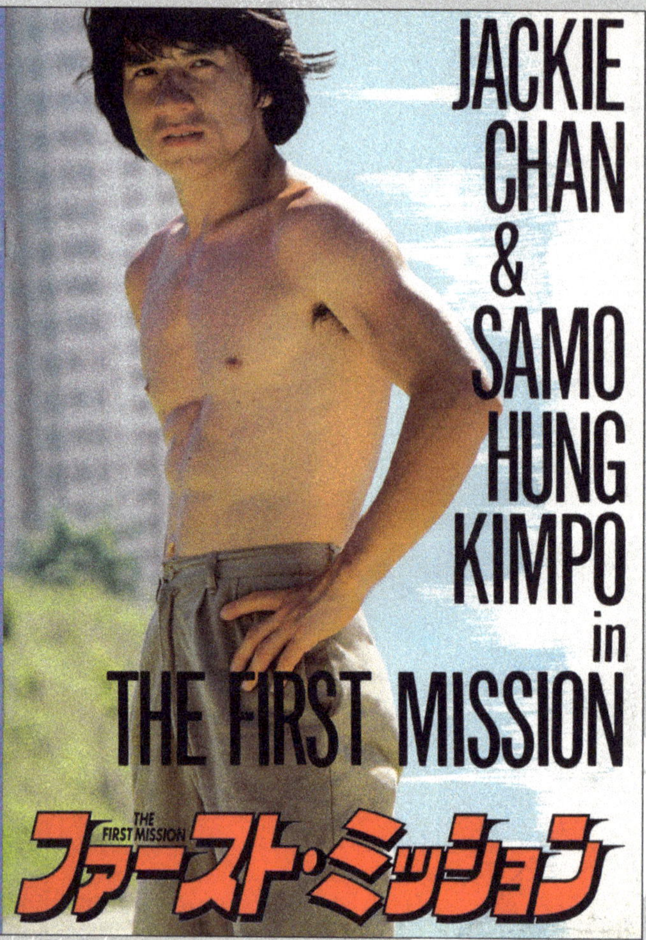

七福星 SEVEN LUCKY STARS

特捜刑事マッスル…ジャッキー・チェン
キッド…ハン・キンポー
特捜刑事リッキー…ユン・ピョウ
クレージー…リチャード・ウン
ちび…エリック・ツァン
びげ…フォン・ツイフェン
虫めがね…ジョニー・シャム
二枚目…チャーリー・チン
フラワー刑事…シベール・フー
ワン…ロザムンド・クァン
線乱屋…倉田保昭
特捜刑事ラッキー…アンディ・ラウ
プレイボーイ…ミウ・キウ・ワイ
美女のインストラクター…ミッシェル・キング

製作総指揮…レイモンド・チョウ
製作…レナード・ホー/エリック・ツァン
監督…ハン・キンポー
脚本…バリー・ウォン
撮影…アーサー・ウォン/ジョニー・クー
武術指導…ユン・ピョウ
主題歌「無問題」…唄/ジャッキー・チェン
オリジナルサウンドトラック盤(ワーナー・パイオニア)

ゴールデン・ハーベスト作品
配給…東映株式会社

THE END

REIGEN DOHSHI 2
霊幻道士2 キョンシーの息子たち!

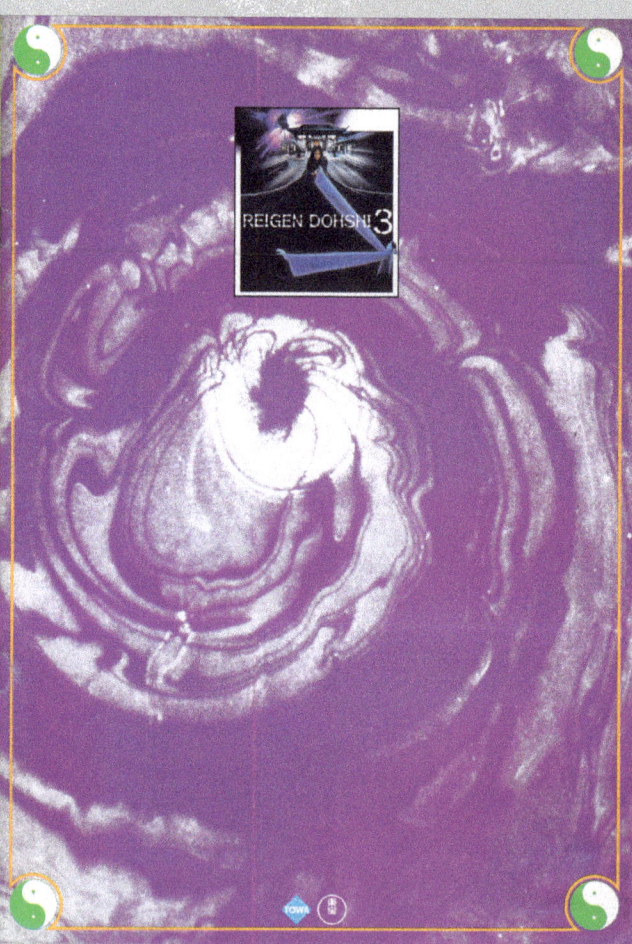

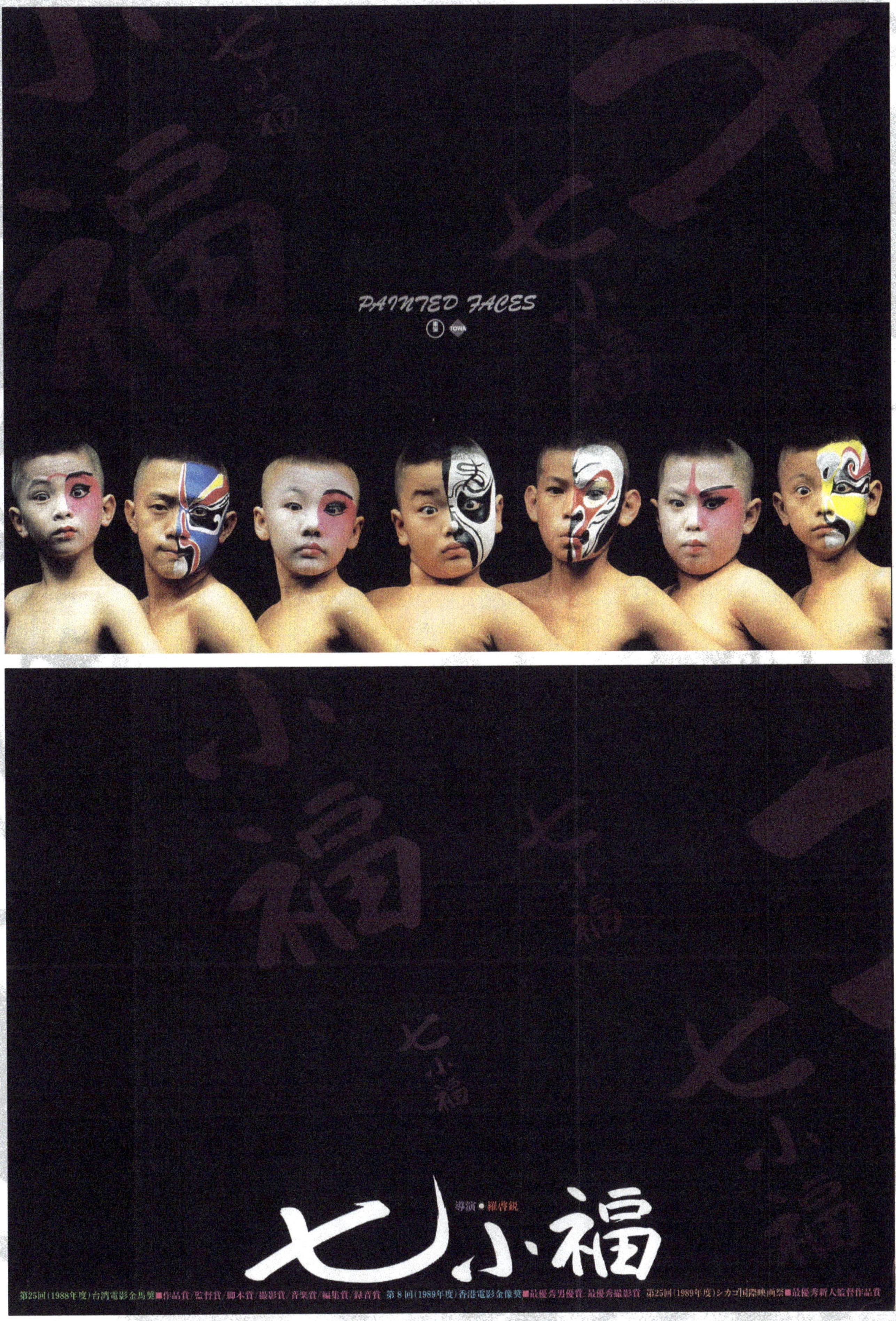

PAINTED FACES

七小福

導演●羅啓銳

第25回(1988年度)台灣電影金馬獎■作品賞/監督賞/脚本賞/撮影賞/音樂賞/編輯賞/錄音賞 第8回(1989年度)香港電影金像獎■最優秀男優賞 最優秀撮影賞 第25回(1989年度)シカゴ国際映画祭■最優秀新人監督作品賞

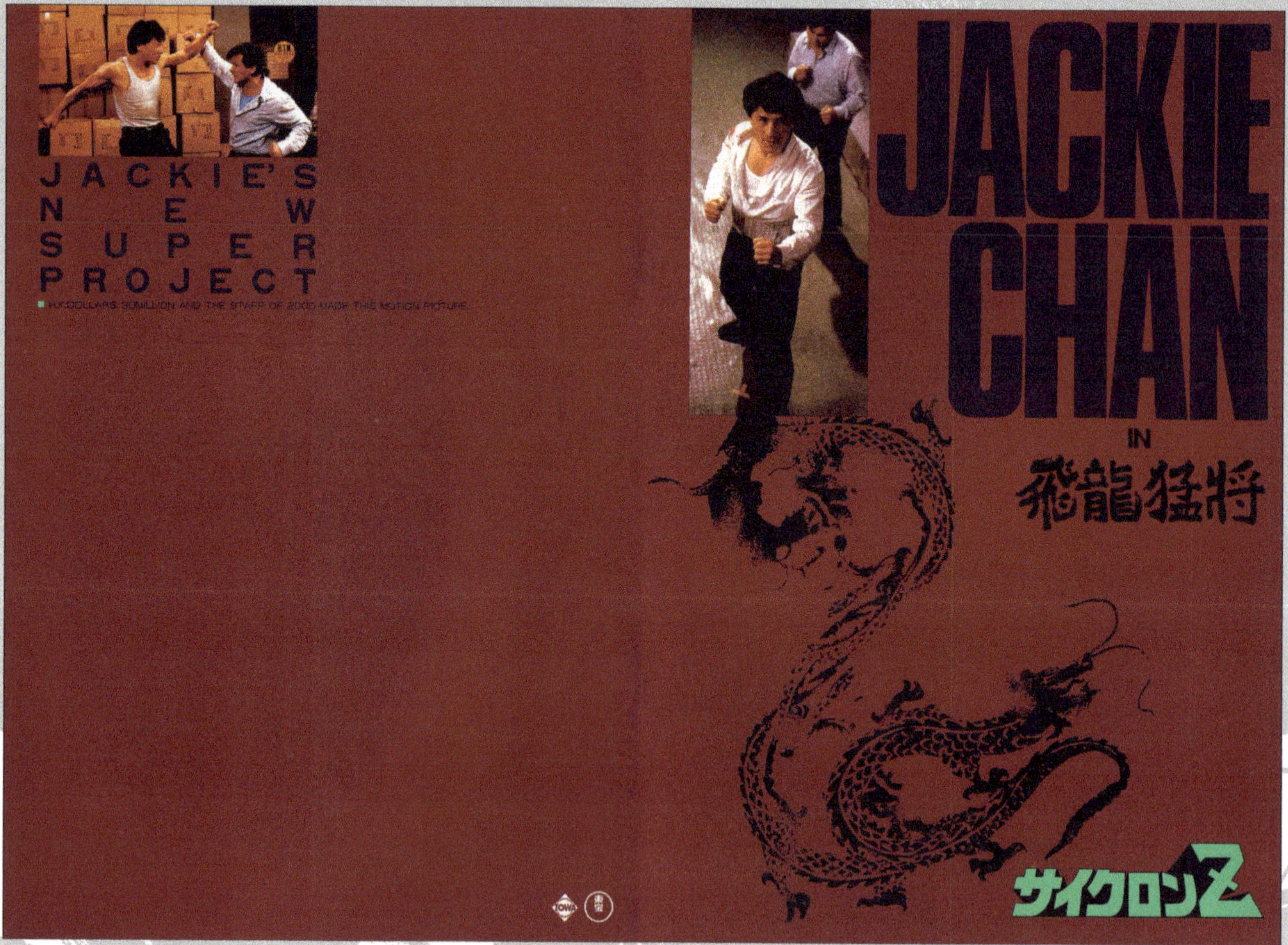
JACKIE'S
NEW
SUPER
PROJECT
H.K.DOLLARS 30MILLION AND THE STAFF OF 2000 MADE THIS MOTION PICTURE.
JACKIE CHAN
IN
飛龍猛将
サイクロンZ

THE SETTING SUN
落陽
にっかつ80周年記念作品
THE SETTING SUN
落陽

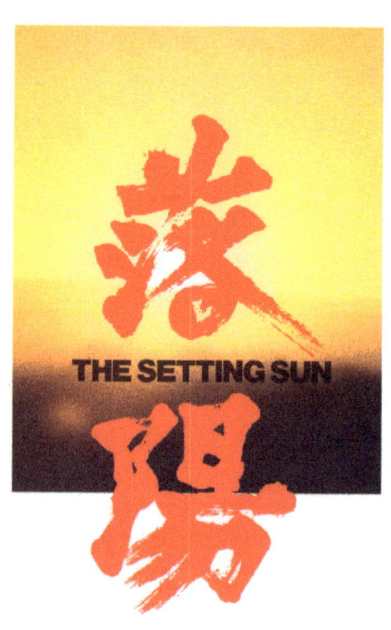

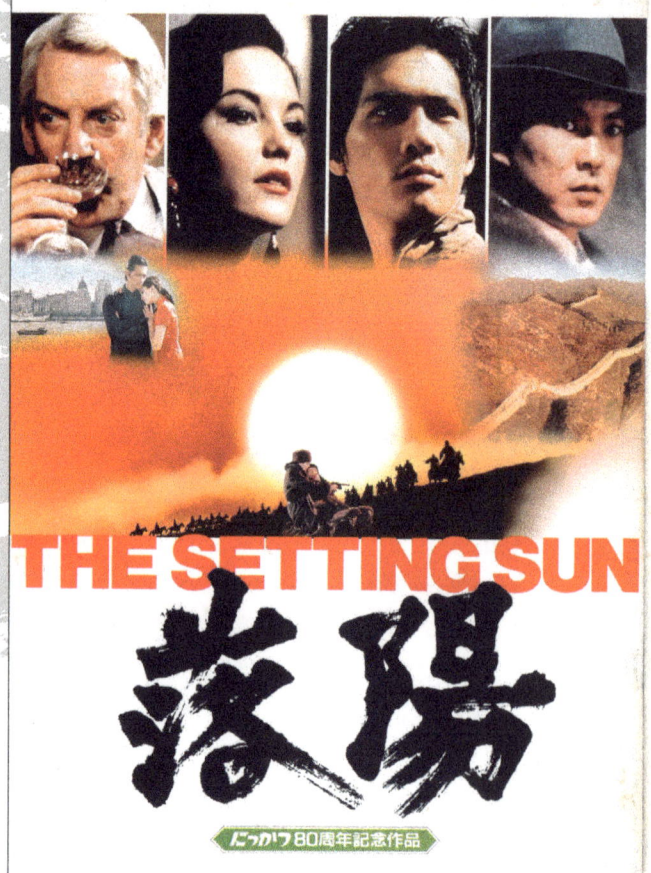

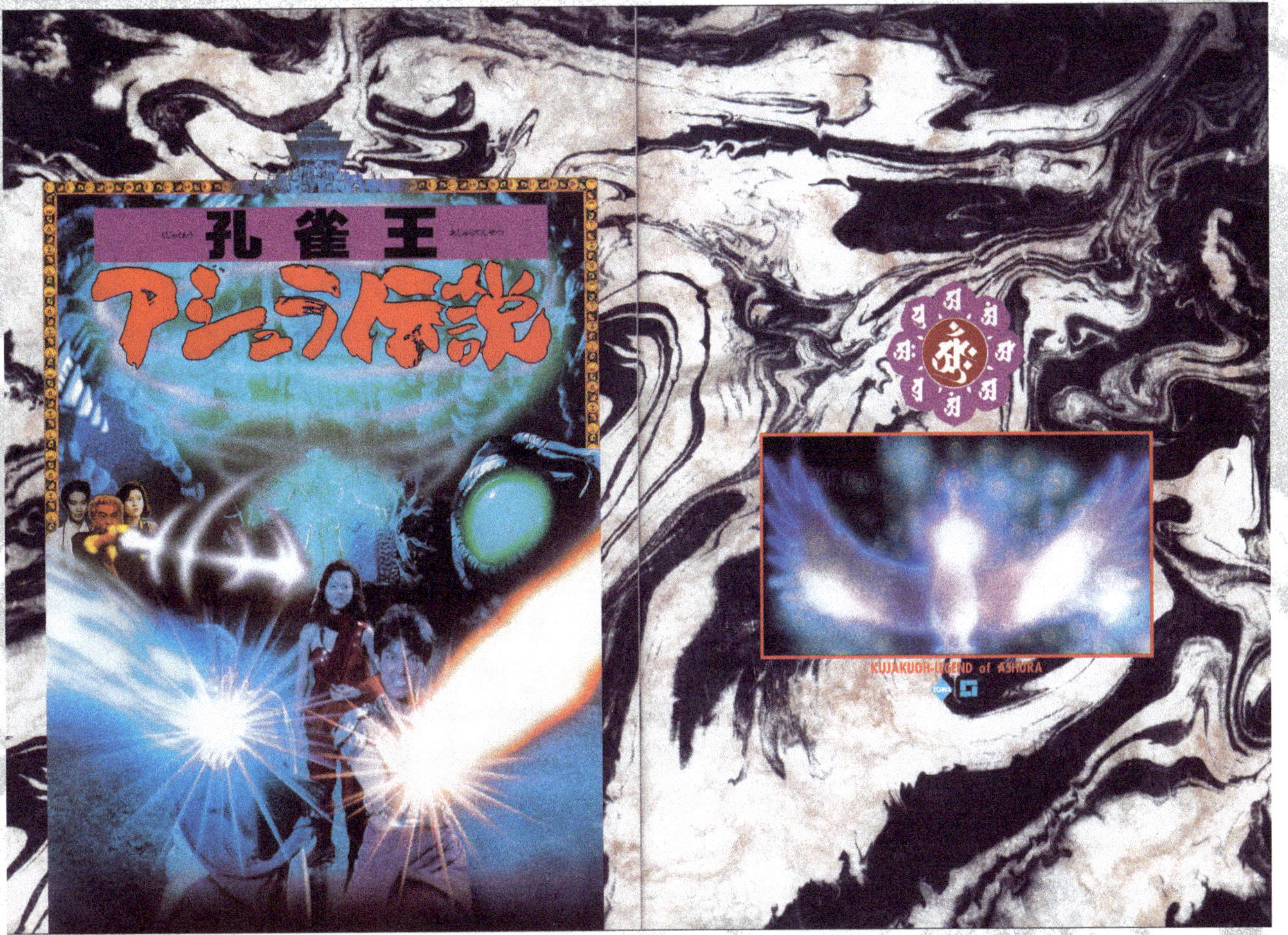

孔雀王
アシュラ伝説
KUJAKUOH-LEGEND of ASHURA

THE BODYGUARD
我的特工爺爺
サモ・ハン is BACK!
おじいちゃんを怒らせないで!
香港映画界のレジェンド、サモ・ハンが
20年ぶりにメガホンを取った愛と感動のアクション巨編!
監督・主演・アクション監督：サモ・ハン
おじいちゃんはデブゴン
THE BODYGUARD
我的特工爺爺

Flyers

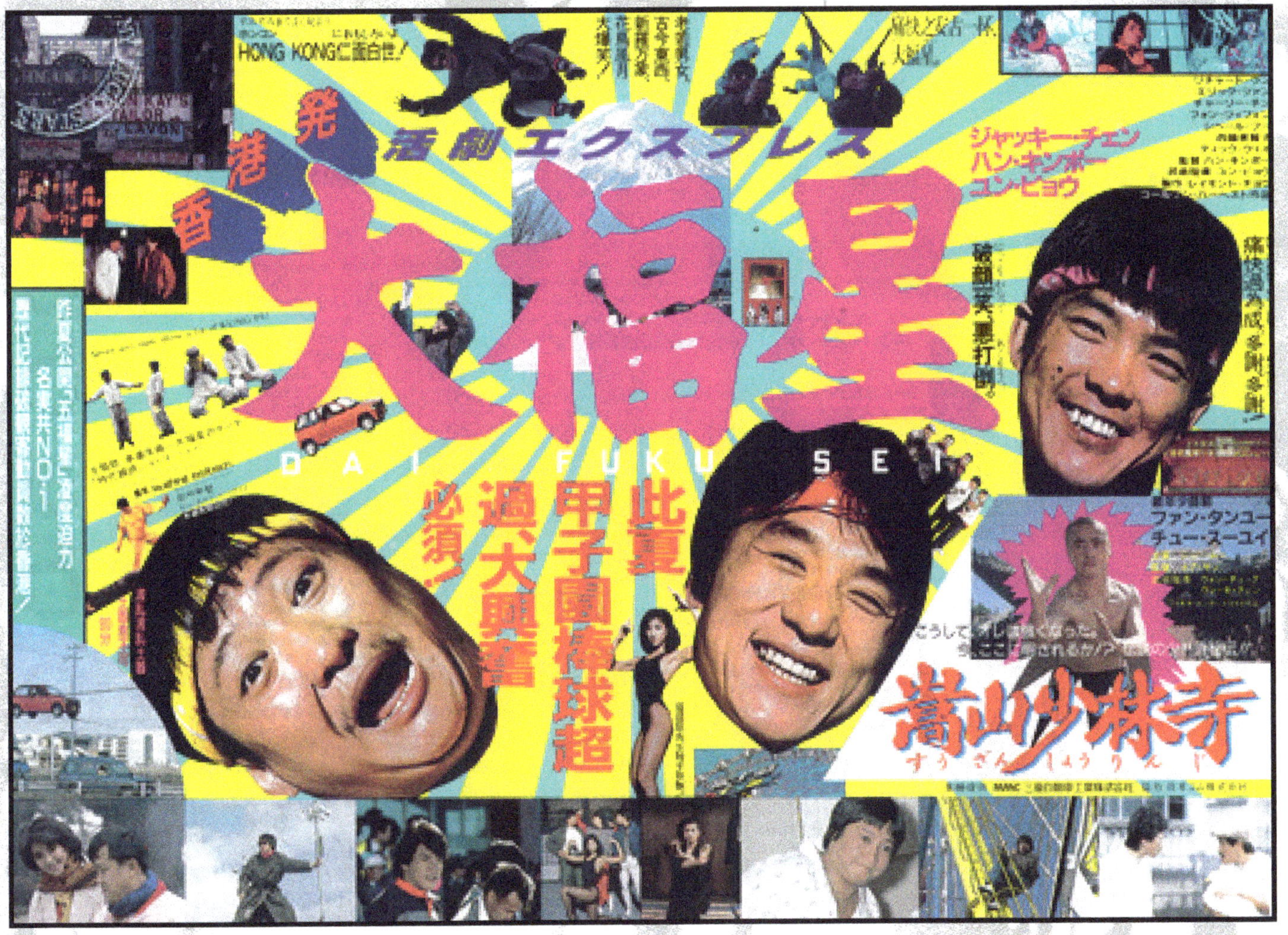

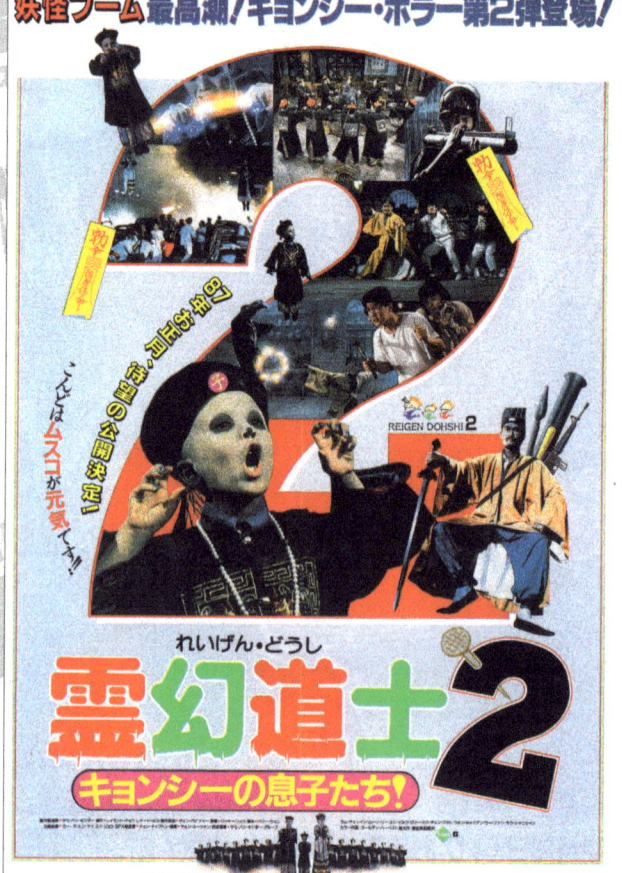

孔雀よ
決して『地獄門』を
開かせてはならぬ
孔雀王

大予言に刻印された"終末への七日間"!
孔雀王
アシュラ伝説

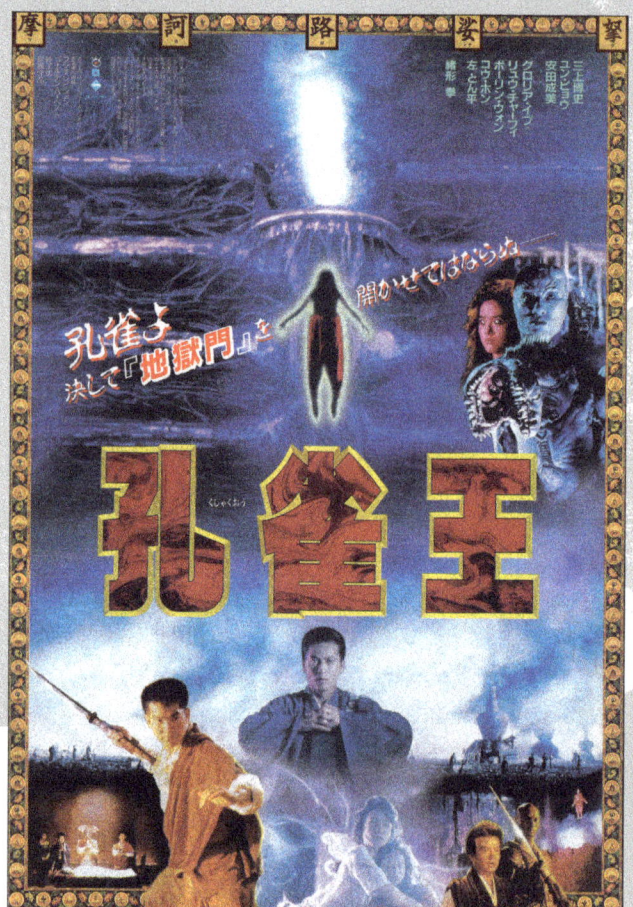

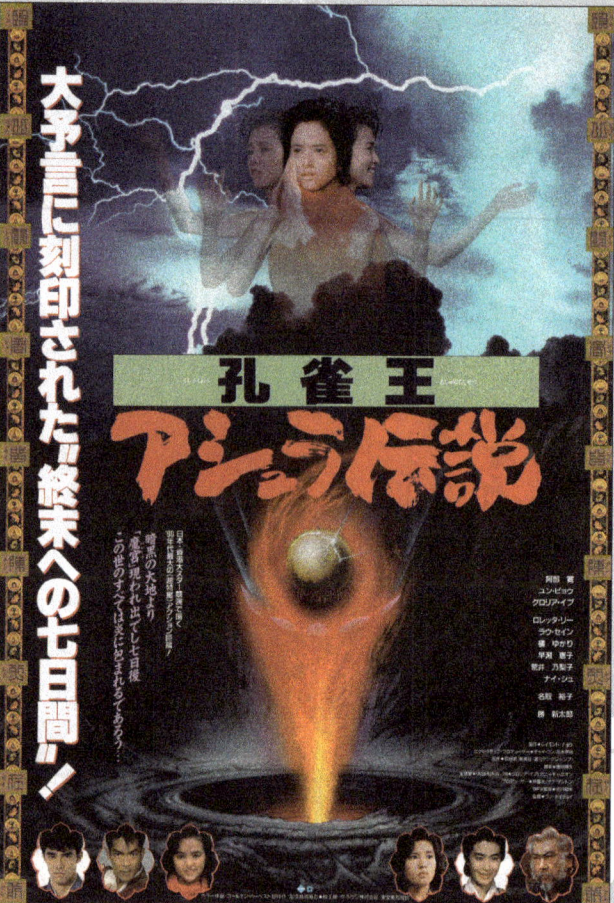

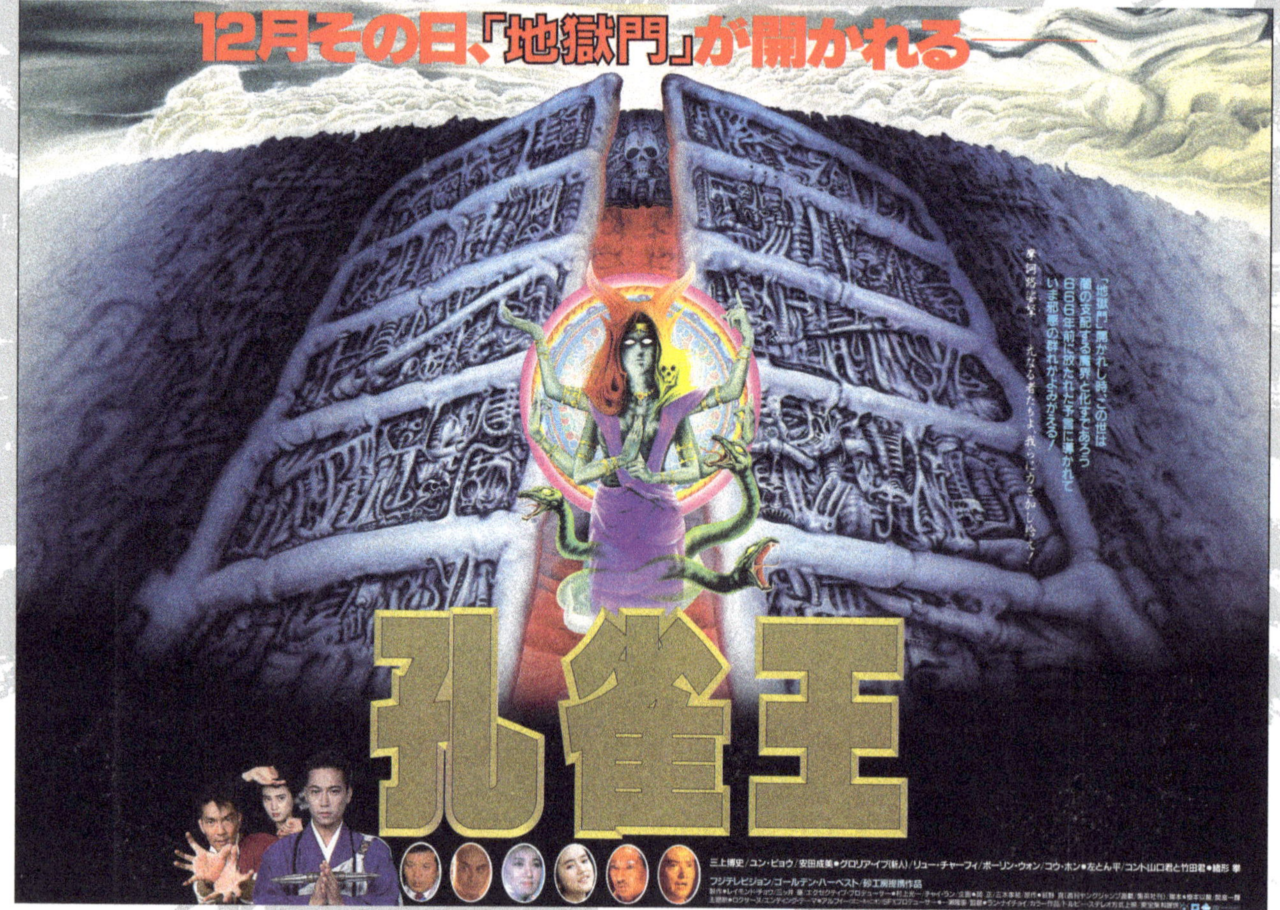

12月その日、「地獄門」が開かれる
孔雀王

LPs

EPs

MAGAZINES

THANK YOU'S

I would like to say a special thank you, to all those involved In making this fantastic bumper issue. Without the people from around the world who took time out to pay their respects, issues like this would never come to fruition.

A special thank you to the following:

Interviews
Cynthia Rothrock
Louis Mandylor
Andy Cheng
Richard Norton
Kelly Hu
Robert Samuels

Contributors
Alan Donkin
Michael Nesbitt
Martin Sandison
Jason McNeil
Mike Leeder
Toby Russell
Cover Art by: Crike99art
Designed by: Tim Hollingsworth

And of course a very special thank you to SAMMO HUNG

Keep the faith

Rick Baker

Kung Fu Ricky